EMPATH

GUIDE TO BETTER EMOTIONAL HEALING AND SPIRITUALITY

Table of contents

Contents

INTRODUCTION

Our social experiences are bewilderingly mind-boggling. They not just include covering layers of full of feeling, conative, and cognitive commitment among self as well as other people. They are likewise profoundly installed in persistently changing situations that shape experiential, emotional, and epistemic types of sharing unmistakable of these experiences—types of sharing that are, like this, further balanced by logical factors, for example, genuine or envisioned gathering enrollment and moving social characters. Also, every one of these social procedures differently influences and feeds back onto the others. This mind-boggling tangle of multi-layered procedures bolsters center social limits like our ability for association, participation, and full of feeling sharing, joint organization, and recognizable social proof. It likewise straightforwardly impacts our ability for empathy: our capacity to see, comprehend, and react to the encounters and conduct of others. Empathy is encouraged—yet in addition, tweaked, one-sided, or even disturbed by—different parts of these procedures. As it were, empathy is a heartily arranged practice, one that is bound up with a rich exhibit of procedures that incorporate not just the elements of our eye to eye commitment yet additionally the mind-boggling conditions in which these commitments create and come to fruition.

Right now, it isn't dubious to state that these central elements of our sociality, which can be extensively subsumed under the names "empathy," "shared feelings," and "social personality," are different and enormously interconnected. Most contemporary savants, cognitive researchers, formative and social therapists, and social neuroscientists working in these regions will promptly buy in any event to the general shapes of this image. It is all the more astonishing, in this way, that little consideration has so far been paid to thoughtfully and methodically explain how these distinctive social procedures may meet and affect each other. Rather, a large portion of the important philosophical, social-logical, and experimental work in the previous decade has concentrated basically on explicit parts of these various components of sociality in segregation and has not methodically tended to their interconnection.

This extraordinary issue moves the focal point of these discussions by investigating joins among philosophical and psychological research on empathy, shared feelings, and social character.

This book focuses more on human relationships, feelings, mindfulness, etc. Additionally, inserted right now:

- What psychological systems support instrumental aiding and prosocial conduct?

- To what degree does empathy empower the joint organization, emotional sharing, and the rise and support of gathering and social personality? What job does pre-intelligent or subpersonal process play here? Shouldn't something be said about story rehearses?

- Conversely, how do shared feelings, social personality, or gathering participation regulate or inclination empathic understanding at both the relational and the intergroup level?

- What is the nature of distinguishing social proof, and how does our capacity to empathize with a specific another affect our relationship with a gathering?

- Do complex types of distinguishing social proof (e.g., bunch ID) surmise increasingly essential types of empathy or other relational procedures like joint consideration and impersonation? What exclusionary and ingroup/outgroup components are included?

- What job do the interrelated socio-psychological procedures of stereotyping, social (self-) arrangement, depersonalization, or dehumanization play here, and how does self-distance factor in?

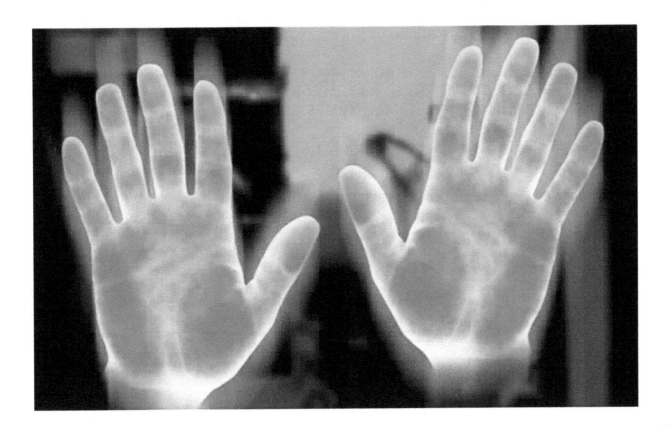

EMPATHY

Empathy is understanding individuals' sentiments, going into their universe of emotions, and giving them that we feel along these lines. Empathy is, at its least difficult, attention to the sentiments and feelings of others. It is a major components of Emotional Intelligence, the connection among self as well as other people since it is the means by which we as people comprehend what others are encountering as though we were feeling it ourselves.

Empathy goes a long way past compassion, which may be considered 'feeling for' somebody. Empathy, rather, is 'feeling with' that individual, using a creative mind.

Emotional Intelligence

Huge numbers of us know about IQ (Intelligence Quotient). Intended to quantify scholarly intelligence, it gives a score from a progression of tests. Higher IQs demonstrate better cognitive capacities, or the capacity to learn and comprehend. Individuals with higher IQs are bound to do well scholastically without applying a similar measure of mental exertion as those with lower IQ scores.

A sensible presumption, in this way, is individuals with higher IQs will be increasingly fruitful at work and through life. This supposition has been demonstrated inaccurate – there is something else entirely to progress than basically being 'shrewd.'

Emotional Intelligence (EI or once in a while EQ – Emotional Quotient).

Advantages of Higher Emotional Intelligence

- People with higher emotional intelligence think that it's simpler to shape and keep up relational connections and to 'fit in' to gather circumstances.

- People with higher emotional intelligence are additionally better at understanding their own psychological state, which can incorporate overseeing pressure viably and being more reluctant to experience the ill effects of melancholy.

There is no connection between's IQ and EI scores.

As it were, scholastic fitness (IQ) has no association with how individuals comprehend and manage their feelings and the feelings of others (EI). This bodes well: we've all met sharp individuals who, in any case, had no clue about how to manage individuals, and the switch.

A few people have high IQs and low emotional intelligence and the other way around, while a few people score exceptionally on both, and some don't.

Level of intelligence and emotional intelligence endeavor to quantify various types of human intelligence; alongside the character, these measures make up a person's mind.

Emotional intelligence is one piece of the human mind that we can create and improve by learning and rehearsing new abilities. You can take in progressively about these aptitudes from the numerous pages here at the Skills you need. Level of intelligence and character are increasingly static measures and prone to remain sensibly consistent all through life (even though you can build up your capacity to finish IQ tests effectively).

Understanding Other People

On the off chance that you solicited a gathering from individuals to characterize 'empathy,' you would in all likelihood locate that one of the main things that anybody proposed was 'a capacity to comprehend others' sentiments.'

Nonetheless, understanding others is something other than detecting others' sentiments and feelings. It additionally implies taking a certified enthusiasm for them and their interests.

Understanding Others - The Skills You Need

Individuals who are acceptable at understanding others:

- Pick up emotional prompts, regularly from body language, manner of speaking, and other non-verbal elements of communication. For increasingly about this, see our pages on Non-Verbal Communication and Body Language.

- Listen well to what individuals are stating, effectively checking their understanding. You may think that it's accommodating to peruse our pages on Active Listening, Clarifying, and Reflecting.

At the point when individuals talk, listen totally. The vast majority never tune in.

A great many people don't tune in with the plan to comprehend; they tune in with the purpose to answer.

- Show affectability towards others, and comprehend their viewpoints. They are mindful so as not to give offense by saying or doing an inappropriate thing, and know that not every person has a similar perspective. Our pages on Being Polite, Tact, and Diplomacy and Intercultural Awareness may assist you with developing this region of your abilities. If you are battling with the harmony between truth, trustworthiness, and amiability, you may discover our pages on Truthfulness and Balancing Honesty and Politeness accommodating.

- Help others properly in light of their understanding of their needs and feelings.

Bits of knowledge from Understanding Others

Creating empathy, and especially the aptitude of understanding others isn't only imperative to your relational connections. It can likewise have a lot more extensive effect.

For instance, in the US, specialists who listen cautiously to their patients are considerably less liable to be sued.

Essential consideration specialists who had never been sued were seen as many preferable communicators over their friends.

The Importance of Sincerity

It is conceivable to imagine that you comprehend individuals' emotions and, all the more especially, their interests. Deals staff regularly do this to attempt to build up affinity with clients.

Nonetheless, as people, we are modified to identify and disdain deviousness.

Your falsification most would agree, will be identified by everyone around you, presumably through unobtrusive indications in your body language, or maybe in a reaction to an unforeseen inquiry.

The other individual may not know about distinguishing it, however, will feel awkward with the discussion that you have attempted to strike up, or with what you are stating, and find that they don't generally confide in you.

As such, this 'bogus empathy' will be counter-gainful.

Attempting to control feelings can reverse discharge on the culprit, and may well not be advantageous. The individuals who are truly empathetic will get an altogether different reaction.

Empathy Avoidance and Empathy Overload

There are two parts of understanding others and being keen on their interests that, as a major aspect of empathy, merit investigating further.

The primary, empathy shirking, is a purposeful absence of empathy, which may be called 'emotional musical inability.'

Absolute empathy evasion is probably not going to be solid for your long haul connections, yet having the option to close down a portion of your empathetic reaction might be useful in specific situations. For instance:

- At Home. Kids need to get certain inoculations. In their initial scarcely any long periods of life, they have a few inoculations, once in a while a few at once. Having a needle stuck into their legs damages, and infants shout when it occurs.

Guardians, be that as it may, need to cinch down on their prompt reaction and perceive the long haul advantages of inoculation, in maintaining a strategic distance from genuine sicknesses, as opposed to concentrating on the momentary pain of the youngster.

- At Work. Supervisors liable for making redundancies should have the option to use sound judgment. They are probably not going to have the option to do as such in the event that they are battling with their own emotional reaction to the trouble of people around them.

- While it is significant that they stay mindful of the sentiments of those included, they must have the option to offset that with the utilization of reason and rationale and not be overpowered.

- In Healthcare. A specialist performing crisis medical procedure on somebody who has had genuine wounds in a streetcar crash should have the option to utilize every one of their aptitudes to attempt to fix the harm or cut away if important to spare the patient's life. They can't invest energy thinking about how this may cause the patient to feel.

In any case, after the activity is finished, and the individual is wakeful, they have to clarify their activities and help the patient to begin to grapple with whatever has occurred. They have to stay mindful of their patient as an individual, with sentiments and concerns and react fittingly.

Empathy over-burden at times happens when individuals are presented to troublesome and upsetting data.

In such circumstances, individuals can get themselves unfit to manage their own emotional reaction to the circumstance. This can occur, for instance, in the event that you locate that a companion is genuinely sick. You need to help and bolster them, yet you are too disturbed to even think about doing so. It is additionally an issue that can emerge for individuals working in callings like prescription, nursing, and social work.

The best approach to oversee conceivable empathy over-burden is to chip away at your self-regulation, and especially your self-control. With developed self-regulation, you will have the option to deal with your own feelings and react suitably to those of others.

Understanding Others isn't 'Delicate.'

We frequently talk about 'delicate abilities,' and there is no doubt that empathy and understanding others are significant delicate aptitudes.

There is, be that as it may, literally nothing delicate, in the feeling of 'simple,' about understanding others' interests and emotions. Nor is it 'delicate' in the feeling of not being extreme: the best directors are empathetic, yet not 'delicate' in their group.

Understanding others doesn't imply that you need to concur with their emotions or perspective. Rather, it implies that you perceive their perspective and acknowledge that it is not quite the same as yours.

You may even now need to do troublesome things that others don't concur with. However, ideally, both you and they get that.

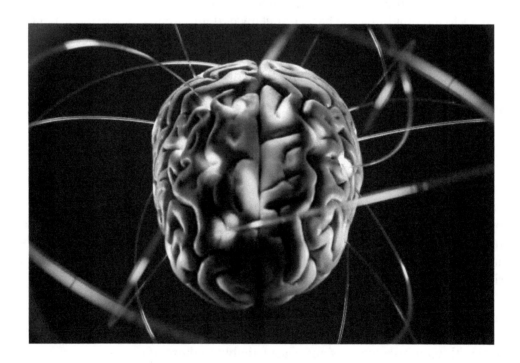

TYPES OF EMPATHY

Empathy IS significant what's more, the sort of empathy that you express or experience matters also.

Cognitive, Emotional, and Compassionate empathy all show in various manners. Thinking about your own encounters at home, at the workplace, or with loved ones, it most likely won't take long for you to see the various sorts in your own life. There are copious models on TV, in governmental issues, and in mainstream society to draw from as well.

Fundamentally, there are three significant kinds of empathy to be specific:

1. Cognitive empathy

2. Emotional empathy

3. Compassionate empathy

Likewise, there are other two kinds of empathy; they are,

A. Somatic empathy

B. Spiritual empathy

The Three Kinds of Empathy Explained: Emotional, Cognitive, And Compassionate

Do you know what the three sorts of empathy are and how to communicate them? Empathy is a must-learn aptitude that carries more simplicity to your life and connections!

When an understudy discloses to you, they're overpowered, or your accomplice returns home with terrible news from work—do you react with empathy? Or then again, do you respond?

All in all, how might you react if your accomplice got back home overpowered with dread, bitterness, and outrage and disclosed to you she'd quite recently lost her employment? The perfect is to react keenly and empathetically.

The thing is, not all empathy appears to be identical. Much the same as not all pity is the equivalent, or bliss, or dread.

This is a point we're enthusiastic about at Heartmanity, particularly on the grounds that empathy is so essential to emotional intelligence (EQ) and interfacing with your loved ones and work with.

Consider the satisfaction of getting off work on Friday versus the delight of a wedding or the contorted joy of Schadenfreude, German, for the pleasure in another, 's incident.

Empathy has various aspects, as well. Truth be told, empathy additionally originates from a German word, Einfühlung, signifying "feeling in." And similarly, as there are numerous approaches to feel, there are different approaches to encounter empathy.

The three kinds of empathy that therapists have characterized are: Cognitive, Emotional, and Compassionate.

As an aside, it's significant that empathy is a moderately new thought and as yet being characterized by social and cognitive therapists.

Empathy IS significant. Furthermore, the kind of empathy that you express or experience matters also.

Cognitive, Emotional, and Compassionate empathy all show in various manners. Thinking about your own encounters at home, at the workplace, or with loved ones, it most likely won't take long for you to see the various kinds in your own life. There are abundant models on TV, in governmental issues, and in mainstream society to draw from as well.

Cognitive Empathy

By definition: "Basically knowing how the other individual feels and what they may be thinking. Some of the time called the point of view taking".

What it's worried about: Thought, understanding, mind.

Advantages: Helps in arrangements, inspiring others, understanding assorted perspectives.

Entanglements: Can be detached from or overlook profound feelings; doesn't place you from another's point of view in a felt sense.

Cognitive Empathy is about the idea as much as the feeling.

It is characterized by knowing, understanding, or appreciating on a scholarly level. As a large portion of us know, to comprehend bitterness isn't a similar thing as feeling dismal.

I speculate that in the event that I got back home a miracle about losing employment, my own accomplice would react along these lines. Similarly that a specialist can take a gander at a wiped outpatient and attempt to comprehend the pieces of the disease as opposed to plunge into the patient's feelings—cognitive empathy reacts to an issue with intellectual competence. My life partner, a designer, and pilot transforms his cerebrum into high rigging in circumstances like this. You could state it's the manner in which a few people are wired to comprehend feelings as far as why they bode well for people in specific circumstances.

This kind of empathy can be an enormous resource in conditions where you have to "get inside someone else's head" or cooperate with thoughtfulness and understanding. We talk about this in our blog, "Emotional Intelligence and Empathy in Leadership." On the other hand, cognitive empathy is somehow or another like blending apples and oranges. To really comprehend someone else's emotions, don't you, in some sense, must have the option to feel them yourself? The individuals who respond with Cognitive Empathy hazard appearing to be cold or separated.

Emotional Empathy

By definition: "when you feel genuinely alongside the other individual, just as their feelings were infectious."

What it's worried about: emotions, physical sensation, reflect neurons in mind.

Advantages: Helps in close relational connections and professions like instructing, promoting the board, and HR.

Traps: Can be overpowering, or unseemly in specific conditions.

Emotional Empathy, much the same as is sounds, includes legitimately feeling the feelings that someone else is feeling. You've likely known about the expression "empath," which means an individual with the capacity to take on the emotional and mental condition of another completely. The statement that strikes a chord is: "I have a lot of sentiments."

This kind of reaction may appear to be separated from the cerebrum and thinking; however, as Goldman brings up, emotional empathy is quite established in a human's mirror neurons. All creatures have neurons that fire with a specific goal in mind when they see another creature acting, causing them to identify with that activity in their own body and cerebrum. Emotional empathy does precisely that with the sentiments somebody encounters in response to a circumstance.

At the point when your accomplice—or anybody you profoundly love—comes to you in tears, it's a characteristic reaction to feel that pull on your heartstrings. Like crying at a wedding or recoiling when somebody stubs their toe, it's a profound situated, gut response that frequently feels like an instinctive human reaction. Interfacing with another human right now close and can frame a solid bond.

Like Cognitive Empathy, Emotional Empathy has its flip-side. "One drawback of emotional empathy happens when individuals do not have the capacity to deal with their own upsetting feelings," composes Goldman. "[This] can be found in the psychological depletion that prompts burnout." Feeling a lot of cans make even little collaborations overpowering.

Compassionate Empathy

By definition: "With this sort of empathy, we not just comprehend an individual's pickle and feel with them, yet are unexpectedly moved to help, if necessary."

What it's worried about: Intellect, feeling, and activity.

Advantages: Considers the entire individual.

Traps: Few—this is the sort of empathy that we're typically taking a stab at!

Most of the time, Compassionate Empathy is perfect. Cognitive Empathy might be fitting for political or fiscal dealings or specialist's workplaces; Emotional Empathy might be the first reaction in quite a while and for our friends and family; Compassionate Empathy finds some kind of harmony of the two.

Sentiments of the heart and musings of the mind are not contrary energies. Truth be told, they're complicatedly associated. Compassionate Empathy praises that regular association by considering both the felt faculties and scholarly circumstance of someone else.

At the point when your cherished one comes to you in tears, you need to comprehend why she is vexed, and you additionally need to give comfort by partaking as far as she can tell and ideally helping her mend. It's a great deal to deal with!

The majority of us will slant to the other side or the other: all the more reasoning or all, the more believing; all the more fixing or all, the more floundering.

Compassionate Empathy is taking the center ground and utilizing your emotional intelligence to react to the circumstance accurately. Should your accomplice simply be held? Does the circumstance call for snappy activity? Without either turning out to be overpowered by pity or attempting to fix things with coordinations, compassion carries a careful touch to the predicament.

At the point when I consider empathy, I regularly think about a seesaw. Go excessively far into someone else's mind, and do you hazard losing yourself? Abstain from plunging into their reality, and would you say you are passing up an essential piece of the human experience? Is an excess of feeling wrong? Excessively little, harmful?

In all actuality, not all circumstances are the equivalent simply like not a wide range of empathy is the equivalent.

Would you be able to consider one case of each kind of empathy in your own life? Likely more than one. Ideally, you've experienced compassionate empathy sooner or later!

Any kind of empathy takes emotional wellness and practice—simply like any exercise in careful control. At the point when you locate that sweet spot where you can empathize successfully, in the case of exploring a work environment obstacle or soothing a friend or family member, it is completely worth the work.

The Two Other Types of Empathy

For finishing, it merits referencing that a few people recommend that there are two different types of empathy, physical and spiritual.

- **Somatic empathy** is characterized as sympathizing with another person's torment genuinely.

  For instance, in the event that you see somebody hurt, you also may feel physical agony. Episodically, indistinguishable twins once in a while report that they know when different has been harmed, which may be a case of physical empathy. You can see a reverberation of substantial empathy, for instance, in the event that somebody is hit in the stomach with a ball during a games game, and a couple of the observers may twofold over as though they also had been hit.

- **Spiritual empathy** is characterized as an immediate association with a 'higher being' or awareness.

  It is equivalent to 'edification' in the eastern philosophical custom and viewed as attainable through meditation.

THE ELEMENTS OF EMPATHY

There are various classes related to the elements of empathy; they are distinguished as the five key elements of empathy.

1. Understanding Others

2. Developing Others

3. Having a Service Orientation

4. Leveraging Diversity

5. Political Awareness

1. Understanding Others

This is maybe what a great many people comprehend by 'empathy': "detecting others' emotions and points of view, and taking a functioning enthusiasm for their interests." The individuals who do this:

- Tune into emotional signals. They listen well, and furthermore focus on non-verbal communication, getting unobtrusive prompts subliminally.

- Show affectability and comprehend others' points of view.

- Are ready to help others dependent on their understanding of those individuals' needs and emotions.

All these are abilities which can be grown, however, just on the off chance that you wish to do as such. A few people may turn off their emotional receiving wires to abstain from being overwhelmed by the sentiments of others.

.

Understanding Others - The Skills You Need

Individuals who are acceptable at understanding others:

• Pick up emotional prompts, frequently from body language, manner of speaking, and other non-verbal elements of communication.

• Listen well to what individuals are stating, effectively checking their understanding.

At the point when individuals talk, listen totally. A great many people never tune in.

A great many people don't tune in with the expectation to comprehend; they tune in with the plan to answer.

• Show affectability towards others, and comprehend their points of view. They are mindful so as not to give offense by saying or doing an inappropriate thing, and know that not every person has a similar purpose of view. If you are battling with the harmony between truth, trustworthiness, and consideration, you may discover our pages on Truthfulness and Balancing Honesty and Politeness accommodating.

• Help others suitably in view of their understanding of their needs and feelings.

Bits of knowledge from Understanding Others

Creating empathy, and especially the ability to understanding others, isn't only imperative to your relational connections. It can likewise have a lot more extensive effect.

2. Developing Others

Creating others implies following up on their necessities and concerns, and helping them to create to their maximum capacity. Individuals with aptitudes right now:

• Reward and commendation individuals for their qualities and achievements, and give productive criticism intended to concentrate on the most proficient method to improve.

• Provide tutoring and instructing to help other people to create to their maximum capacity.

• Provide extending assignments that will assist their groups with developing.

3. Having a Service Orientation

Principally focused on work circumstances, having an assistance direction implies putting the necessities of clients first, and searching for approaches to improve their fulfillment and dedication.

Individuals who have this methodology will 'go the additional mile' for clients. They will really comprehend clients' needs and make a special effort to help meet them.

Right now, it can turn into a 'confided in counsel' to clients, building up a long haul connection among client and association. This can occur in any industry and any circumstance.

There are numerous non-work circumstances that expect us to help other people here and there, where putting their requirements community stage may empower us to see the circumstance distinctively and maybe offer increasingly valuable help and help.

4. Utilizing Diversity

Utilizing decent variety implies having the option to make and create openings through various types of individuals, perceiving and commending that we as a whole carry something other than what's expected to the table.

Utilizing decent variety doesn't imply that you treat everybody in the very same manner, yet that you tailor the manner in which you communicate with others to meet with their requirements and emotions.

Individuals with this ability to regard and relate well to everybody, paying little heed to their experience. When in doubt, they consider decent variety to be a chance, understanding that assorted groups work far superior to groups that are progressively homogeneous.

Individuals who are acceptable at utilizing decent variety additionally challenge narrow mindedness, predisposition, and stereotyping when they see it, making an environment that is deferential towards everybody.

5. Political Awareness

Numerous individuals see 'political' abilities as manipulative, yet in its best sense, 'political' signifies detecting and reacting to a gathering's emotional inclinations and force connections.

Political mindfulness can assist people with navigating hierarchical connections adequately, permitting them to accomplish where others may already have fizzled.

Political mindfulness is a key segment in empathy, which thusly is a piece of Emotional Intelligence.

A few pundits have proposed that political mindfulness is about affectability to open approach and government, and the motivation driving lawmakers.

In any case—and positively in a sense wherein it is utilized in Emotional Intelligence—political mindfulness is tied in with understanding the 'flows,' or shrouded motivation, in an association, and especially the force connections.

Numerous individuals may have been put off being politically mindful by observing individuals 'wading into controversy's or attempting to control others, utilizing political strategies. Be that as it may, utilized astutely and well, political mindfulness is a power for good, and for completing things in associations, and it is a basic aptitude throughout everyday life.

Authoritative Politics and Political Awareness

Authoritative governmental issues—which happen in any gathering, group, or association, regardless of whether social, business, or deliberate—is an expression used to depict the force connections of the gathering.

At the end of the day:

• How do things truly complete around here?

• Who truly has the ability to decide?

• Who follows up on those choices?

Authoritative legislative issues have almost no to do with the authority hierarchical chain of command, and everything to do with individuals, specifically their connections, characters, and past experience.

Political mindfulness is essentially an understanding of these 'power networks' and a capacity to explore them, and hence complete things.

Political mindfulness is firmly connected to Commercial Awareness, then again, actually where business mindfulness is primarily centered around the outside condition of the association, political mindfulness is increasingly about the inner condition.

Empathy, Sympathy, and Compassion

There is a significant qualification between empathy, compassion, and compassion.

Both compassion and compassion are tied in with feeling for somebody: seeing their misery and understanding that they are languishing. Compassion has made on an element of movement that is inadequate in compassion. However, the foundation of the words is equivalent.

Empathy, on the other hand, is tied in with encountering those affections for yourself, as though you were that individual through the intensity of a creative mind.

WHO IS AN EMPATH?

The term empath originates from empathy, which is the capacity to comprehend the encounters and sentiments of others outside of your own point of view.

State your companion simply lost their pooch of 15 years. Empathy is the thing that permits you to comprehend the degree of agony she's experiencing, regardless of whether you've never lost a darling pet.

However, as an empath, you make things a stride further. You really sense and feel feelings as though they're your very own piece understanding. As it were, another person's agony and joy become your torment.

What's more, satisfaction.

An empath is somebody who is profoundly mindful of the feelings of everyone around them, to the level of feeling those feelings themselves. The Empaths see the world uniquely unlike others; they're distinctly mindful of others, their agony focuses, and what they need emotionally.

In any case, it's not simply feelings, empaths can feel physical agony, as well — and can regularly detect somebody's aims or where they're coming from. As it were, empaths appear to get on a large number of the lived understanding of people around them.

Numerous profoundly sensitive individuals (HSPs) are likewise empaths — yet there might be a distinction among empaths and HSPs. Having a high level of empathy is only one of the four attributes that make somebody an HSP, and HSPs are sensitive to numerous sorts of upgrades, notwithstanding feelings. All things considered, most empaths are exceptionally sensitive, yet not all profoundly sensitive individuals are fundamentally empaths.

Indications of an Empath

1. You take on other people groups' feelings as your own

This is the work of art, the number one characteristic of an empath. Regardless of what another person close to you is feeling, regardless of whether they figure they aren't indicating it, you're probably going to get on it right away. Yet, more than that: you may really feel the feeling as though it were your own, basically "engrossing" it or wiping it up.

How precisely this function is a subject of some discussion. Be that as it may, we do realize that individuals who have significant levels of empathy additionally have exceptionally dynamic mirror neurons — the piece of the mind that peruses emotional prompts from others and makes sense of what they may be thinking or feeling. At the end of the day, in case you're an empath, all things considered, you can get on minor changes in articulation, body language, or manner of speaking that others miss — and promptly sense what the individual is feeling.

Those equivalent dynamic mirror neurons, in any case, imply that you essentially live through the inclination as though it were your own. That can be an incredible blessing, yet in addition, debilitating and overpowering now and again.

2. Here and there you experience abrupt, overpowering feelings when you're out in the open

It's not simply in a one-on-one discussion where you sense the feelings of others. It can occur whenever when there are others around, and all of a sudden.

In case you're an empath, it very well may be trying to go into open spaces, since you may out of nowhere end up loaded up with a feeling that left "no place" — or, all the more precisely, from another person in the region.

3. The "vibe" of a room matters to you — a great deal

Maybe obviously, empaths are very sensitive to the "vibe" or air of their environment. At the point when encompassed by harmony and quiet, they thrive, in light of the fact that they take on those characteristics inside themselves. For a similar explanation, spots of magnificence can be transformative for empaths, regardless of whether it's a calm nursery, a flawless room, or the corridors of an exhibition hall. In like manner, disorganized or discouraging situations will rapidly haul the energy out of an empath.

4. You comprehend where individuals are coming from

Empaths clarifies this is the center quality of an empath — significantly more so than retaining the feelings of others. All things considered, empaths can learn not to ingest feelings to such an extent, and some empaths infrequently "retain" them by any stretch of the imagination. In any case, all empaths can instinctively detect what somebody is attempting to communicate, in any event, when they're making some hard memories getting it out.

Empathy, all things considered, is in a general sense about understanding and interfacing with others. Furthermore, that is sensing where individuals are coming from.

5. Individuals go to you for exhortation

With such understanding, empaths are as often as possible searched out by their companion for guidance, backing, and consolation. It helps that empaths likewise will, in general, be acceptable audience members, and will frequently calmly trust that somebody will say what they have to state and afterward react from the heart.

In the event that this seems like you, you presumably realize that it very well may be hard on occasion, as well — individuals don't generally acknowledge the amount of your energy it takes for you to be the audience an exhortation provider, and a few people underestimate it.

6. Grievous or rough occasions on TV can totally debilitate you

In case you're an empath, it doesn't make a difference that a frightful occasion isn't transpiring, you despite everything, feel it through your whole existence. You may appear to "live through" the agony of loss of the occasion yourself, regardless of whether you're a great many miles away — or without a doubt, regardless of whether it's an anecdotal occasion in a show. This response can be totally overpowering now and again.

Empaths, as HSPs, may not do well watching viciousness or human disaster, regardless of whether it's a film that others find grasping.

7. You can't contain your adoration for pets, creatures, or children

Indeed, everybody realizes that children are lovable little supernatural occurrences, and mutts and felines are adorable — however, for you, those emotions appear to be a lot more grounded. You will most likely be unable to help yourself from spouting over somebody's flawless kid, or quickly hunching down to demonstrate some adoration to a doggy. A few people may discover your response "over the top," however, for you, in what capacity can anybody not respond thusly?

From numerous points of view, this is one of the numerous advantages of being an empath. Every one of your emotions, including positive ones, is turned far up.

8. You may feel individuals' physical sicknesses as well — not simply their feelings

At the point when somebody is debilitated or harmed, you may even venture to such an extreme as to feel their infirmity as though it's your own. This doesn't simply mean inclination compassion or worry for them, however having genuine physical sensations like agony, snugness, or irritation in similar zones of the body. Maybe your empathic mind isn't just reflecting what the other individual must understand yet, in addition, anticipating that experience genuinely into your own body.

What's more, it very well may be awkward — in any event, incapacitating. It's presumably not a "blessing" that most empaths love to have. But on the other hand, it's at the base of why empaths are such remarkable guardians. Without this capacity, they wouldn't have the option to really associate with somebody who is in torment, or get them exactly what they have to feel quieter.

It's not astonishing that empaths are attracted to jobs like a medical caretaker, specialist, senior consideration supplier, or healer. On the off chance that you can sympathize with everybody's torment, it would be astounding not to need to take care of business.

9. You can become overpowered in close connections

Connections can be trying for everybody. Be that as it may, envision how much greater those difficulties are the point at which you can detect each and every state of mind, bothering or, truly, even lie from your accomplice. What's more, positive feelings can likewise get overpowering — as though the relationship may "immerse" you. Sound natural?

Yet, it's more than that. When you live respectively, the common condition is likewise an obstacle. A living together accomplice's "energy" is constantly present for an empath, and can nearly feel like an interruption. Empaths see their homes as an asylum where they can escape from the consistent interest on their emotional faculties, and an accomplice changes that.

While some empaths decide to stay single thus, others figure out how to adjust — maybe by having a room that is their private space, or (critical) looking for an accomplice who regards their limits.

10. You're a mobile untruth locator

Indeed, there most likely have been times when somebody effectively misled you… however, that being said, you realized you were conflicting with your gut nature from the beginning. The thing about an empath's capacity to process even the littlest social signs implies that it's practically outlandish for somebody to shroud their actual goals. Regardless of whether you don't know precisely what an individual truly needs, you know whether they're not totally fair — or on the off chance that they appear to be tricky.

11. You can't comprehend why any pioneer wouldn't put their groups first

There are a lot of chiefs and gathering coordinators who essentially don't focus on their group's needs. In case you're an empath, this isn't simply discourteous or irritating — it's a disappointment of initiative.

Mostly, this is on the grounds that empaths can make magnificent pioneers themselves, and when they do, it's consistently by tuning in to their group and joining individuals around shared objectives. Empaths will, in general, be keen and mindful, ensuring each colleague feels heard. The outcome isn't only a more joyful gathering of individuals; it's the creation of better choices by getting all the data.

12. You have a quieting impact on others — and the ability to mend them

It's valid. Similarly, as individuals search out empaths for exhortation, they likewise simply feel more settled in an empath's quality. Truth be told, individuals frequently accidentally search out their most empathic companions during troublesome occasions.

This is something you can create and use to really recuperate individuals, in the feeling of helping them work past genuine emotional stuff and beat unfortunate examples. Be that as it may, you can't do as such on the off chance that you shroud your affectability and empathy — you need to grasp your blessing on the off chance that you truly need to have any kind of effect.

13. You can't see somebody in torment without needing to help

Would you be able to stroll past somebody who's out of luck, without thinking about how you could support them? Do you battle to kill your anxiety for others in light of the fact that "there's an occupation to do"? On the off chance that the appropriate response is no — not in any event, when you're occupied, not in any event, whenever you're hurried — at that point, there's an acceptable possibility you're an empath.

What's more, this is the reason empaths are such an important piece of the astounding kaleidoscope of humankind. For an empath, individuals are the most brilliant things on their radar, and it's outlandish not to see — and react to — the requirements of others. That is actually where an empath's healing capacity originates from, and it's something we could utilize a greater amount of in our reality.

The Difference Between Introverts, Empaths, and Highly Sensitive People

Individuals regularly knot introverts, empaths, and exceptionally sensitive individuals together. Despite the fact that they share some comparative qualities, they're each very unique. So what is simply the distinction — and do you see yourself fitting into at least one of these classifications? How about we investigate.

Introverts

There's been a ton of mindfulness raising about introverts over the previous decade, and the vast majority presently comprehend that being an introvert doesn't really make you modest or asocial. Truth be told, numerous introverts are social individuals who love investing energy with a couple of dear companions. In any case, introverts get depleted rapidly in those social circumstances and need a lot of time alone so as to energize. That is the reason introverts regularly like to remain in or invest energy with only a couple of individuals instead of a major gathering.

Being an introvert is hereditary, and it includes contrasts in how the cerebrum forms dopamine, the "reward" synthetic. Individuals who are conceived as introverts don't feel as compensated by outside boosts, for example, gatherings or talk, and subsequently, they get exhausted in those circumstances generally rapidly. Then again, numerous introverts take profound fulfillment from important exercises like perusing, innovative pastimes, and time for calm thought.

In case you're a profoundly sensitive individual, you're considerably more liable to be an introvert. Dr. Elaine Aron, the creator of The Highly Sensitive Person, appraises that around 70 percent of HSPs are additionally introverts — so it bodes well why they're regularly mistaken for each other.

By and by, you can be an introvert and not be exceptionally sensitive. This would look like being less "in order" with individuals (for HSPs, the most brilliant thing on their radar is others!), just as being less worried by specific kinds of incitement, for example, time pressure, brutal film scenes, dull commotions, and so forth — despite the fact that you despite everything need a lot of alone time.

Furthermore:

♣ About 30 to 50 percent of the populace are introverts

♣ Some introverts are neither empaths nor profoundly sensitive individuals.

♣ Introversion is an all-around considered character quality that is independent of both of the others.

Empaths

Empaths are individuals who are amazingly mindful of the feelings of people around them. To an empath, this doesn't simply want to see others' sentiments; the experience is one of really retaining their feelings. Maybe you're feeling their feelings with them. At the point when overpowered with upsetting feelings, empaths may encounter alarm assaults, sorrow, interminable weakness, and physical side effects that challenge the customary therapeutic finding, she composes.

For empaths, this capacity is both a blessing and a revile. It very well may be hard in light of the fact that numerous empaths feel that they can't "turn it off," or it takes them years to create approaches to turn it down when required. Accordingly, an empath can end up going from superbly glad to overpowered with pressure, tension, or different sentiments just in light of the fact that another person strolled into the room.

Simultaneously, an empath's capacity to assimilate sentiments is their most prominent quality. It permits them to get others and interface profoundly with them. It's additionally what makes them phenomenal overseers, companions, and accomplices — particularly when others comprehend and value their blessing.

Like HSPs, empaths additionally have exceptionally tuned faculties, solid instinctive capacities, and can require time alone to decompress, as indicated by Orloff.

♣ Empaths can be introverts or extroverts.

♣ "Absorbing" feelings in all likelihood occurs by getting on inconspicuous social/emotional signs and afterward disguising them — an oblivious procedure that empaths frequently can't control

♣ Many empaths are likely profoundly sensitive individuals.

Profoundly Sensitive People

Profoundly sensitive individuals are frequently misjudged. It's not unexpected to utilize "sensitive" as though it's a terrible thing, which implies that HSPs, in some cases, get negative criticism. In any case, actually, being profoundly sensitive methods, you process more data about your general surroundings than others do.

For HSPs, that implies:

♣ Processing things profoundly and seeing associations that others don't take note

♣ Sometimes turning out to be overpowered or overstimulated on the grounds that your mind is preparing such a lot of info (particularly in profoundly invigorating situations)

♣ Picking up on emotional prompts, as empaths, and feeling a profound level of empathy for other people

♣ Noticing little and unpretentious things that others don't see (like surfaces and blackout commotions)

As such, being exceptionally sensitive has an emotional measurement to it, and most HSPs would qualify as empaths — they will, in general, feel the feelings of others simply like empaths do. Simultaneously, being an HSP likewise includes being increasingly sensitive to all tangible information, not simply feelings. HSPs can become overpowered in circumstances that are essentially excessively loud, swarmed, or quick-paced, regardless of whether there are explicit feelings to manage or not.

Like contemplation, high affectability has been all around examined. It's to a great extent hereditary and includes a few one of a kind contrasts in mind. It's likewise a sound, typical characteristic shared by up to 20 percent of the populace.

♣ HSPs can be introverts or extroverts.

♣ It's imaginable that most (if not all) HSPs are additionally empaths.

♣ Empaths and HSPs may end up being different sides of a solitary quality as empaths are contemplated more.

The Opposite of an Introvert, Empath, or HSP

Something contrary to an introvert is an extrovert. Extroverts are now and then said to get their energy from social circumstances. They have an any longer "social battery" than introverts, and their cerebrums are wired to get a lot of fulfillment from these circumstances.

Something contrary to empathy or high affectability is now and then said to be narcissism, yet that is just false. Similarly, as being exceptionally sensitive (or empathic) accompanies upsides and downsides, the equivalent is valid for being less sensitive. Less sensitive individuals just aren't as affected by the improvements around them. What's more, that can be a significant attribute in the correct conditions — especially in boisterous, requesting situations like mechanical work locales, the military, and others. These people are not really narcissistic or selfish.

All character qualities exist on purpose. Contemplation, empathy, and high affectability are on the whole significant, worthwhile attributes. Furthermore, the human species does best when we have an assorted populace with a wide range of points of view.

Signs You're a Highly Sensitive Person

An exceptionally sensitive individual (HSP) encounters the world uniquely in contrast to other people. Because of an organic distinction that they're brought into the world with, exceptionally sensitive individuals are increasingly mindful of nuances and procedure data profoundly. This implies they will, in general, be innovative, shrewd, and empathetic, yet it additionally implies they're more inclined than others to stretch and overpower.

In spite of the fact that being profoundly sensitive is totally ordinary — which means, it is anything but a malady or confusion — it's regularly misjudged, on the grounds that solitary 15 to 20 percent of the populace are HSPs.

Is it true that you are a profoundly sensitive individual? On the off chance that you identify with the vast majority of these signs, there's a decent possibility you're an HSP.

Signs You're a Highly Sensitive Person

1. You totally despise brutality and mercilessness of any sort.

Everybody abhors viciousness and cold-bloodedness, however for exceptionally sensitive individuals, seeing or catching wind of it very well may be amazingly disrupting. You may be an HSP in the event that you can't observe terrifying, bloody, or vicious films without getting annoyed or in any event, feeling genuinely sick. So also, you will most likely be unable to stomach a report about creature mercilessness or comparable fierce acts.

2. You're much of the time emotionally depleted from retaining others' sentiments.

Albeit exceptionally sensitive individuals are not really empaths, HSPs tend to "ingest" others' feelings, practically like an empath would. It's not surprising for an HSP to stroll into a room and quickly sense the mind-sets of the individuals in it. That is on the grounds that exceptionally sensitive individuals are mindful of nuances — including outward appearances, body language, and manner of speaking — that others may miss. Pair this with the sensitive individual's normally significant levels of empathy, and it's no big surprise HSPs feel feelings that are not their own. Subsequently, profoundly sensitive individuals will, in general, experience the ill effects of continuous emotional weariness.

3. Time pressure truly shakes you.

In school, planned tests or speed tests made you incredibly on edge — maybe to the point of not having the option to proceed just as you regularly would. As a grown-up, when you have an excessive number of things on your plan for the day and insufficient time to complete them, you feel pushed. HSPs are increasingly sensitive to incitement, and time pressure is no exemption.

4. You pull back regularly.

Regardless of whether you're an introvert or an extrovert, you need a lot of personal time, ideally alone. You frequently end up pulling back to a calm, obscured room toward the finish of a difficult day — so as to bring down your incitement level, mitigate your faculties, and revive.

5. You're nervous.

At the point when somebody sneaks up on you, you bounce like a terrified feline. Numerous HSPs have a high "surprise reflex" on the grounds that even in non-compromising circumstances, their sensory systems are dialed up.

6. You think profoundly.

The foundation of being an HSP is you process data profoundly. This implies you do a lot of thinking about your encounters — more so than others. Lamentably, this additionally implies you're increasingly inclined to negative overthinking. Now and again, you fanatically play occasions again and again in your psyche or winding into restless considerations.

7. You're a searcher.

HSPs look for answers to the unavoidable issues throughout everyday life. They inquire as to why things are how they are and what their job in every last bit of it is. In case you're a profoundly sensitive individual, you may have consistently asked why others aren't as enthralled by the riddles of human instinct and the universe as you seem to be.

8. Unexpected, uproarious clamors alarm you.

For instance, a boisterous cruiser out of nowhere thundering by your window may truly shake you.

9. Your dress issues.

You've generally been sensitive to what you wear. Scratchy texture or prohibitive dress — like jeans with a tight belt or pantyhose — truly bother you. Obviously, none-HSPs may despise these things as well. However, an HSP will cautiously choose their closet to dodge them totally. What's more, if an HSP unintentionally destroys one of these things, the uneasiness may degrade their whole experience.

10. Your agony resistance is less.

Numerous HSPs are progressively sensitive to the agony of different sorts — cerebral pains, body hurts, wounds, and so on — than non-HSPs.

11. Your inward world is alive and present.

Once more, because of your profound handling, you have a rich inward world. As a youngster, you may have had a few fanciful companions, delighted in dream-based play, and were inclined to fantasizing. As a grown-up, you may have distinctively sensible dreams.

12. Change is incredibly upsetting.

HSPs relax because of their schedules, on the grounds that the commonplace is far less animating than something fresh out of the plastic new. Hence, change — both positive and negative — can truly lose HSPs. For instance, when dating another person or finding a new line of work advancement, HSPs may feel as similarly worried as they do thrilled. By and large, HSPs need additional time than others to conform to change.

13. Once in awhile, your condition is your foe.

Correspondingly, moving to another home or voyaging (regardless of whether it's only a "fun" excursion!) can be very hard for you, in light of the fact that your faculties are assaulted with such a lot of new improvements.

14. You're misjudged.

High affectability is frequently mislabeled. You may have been classified "modest" or "on edge," and maybe it was inferred that something wasn't right with you. Thus, numerous HSPs are named as introverts, since introverts and HSPs share numerous attributes, for example, requiring heaps of personal time. Be that as it may, 30 percent of HSPs are really extroverts.

15. You get hangry effectively.

HSPs will, in general, be sensitive to changes in glucose levels, so they may get very "hangry" (hungry + furious) on the off chance that they haven't eaten in some time.

16. Who needs energizers…

… when your sensory system is tightened up to the most elevated level? Some HSPs are sensitive to caffeine and need next to no of it to feel its buzz. Essentially, some HSPs are additionally sensitive to liquor's belongings.

17. Strife is your toxic substance.

When there's strain or contradiction in your cozy connections, you feel it profoundly. Numerous HSPs even report feeling genuinely sick during the struggle. Subsequently, some exceptionally sensitive individuals become struggle avoidant, doing, or saying nearly anything to keep the other individual glad. This is on the grounds that contention harms to such an extent.

18. Analysis is a knife.

Words truly matter to HSPs. Positive words can make them take off, yet cruel words will send them colliding with the ground. Analysis can feel like a knife, and cynicism is harmful to the profoundly sensitive individual's finely-tuned framework.

19. You're honest.

At work and in school, you make a decent attempt not to commit errors. Obviously, this doesn't mean you're great — nobody is! — yet you're continually giving things your best exertion.

20. You're profoundly moved by magnificence.

Fine dinners, rich fragrances, wonderful craftsmanship, or blending songs deeply affect you. You may find that music or certain sounds put you in a close to daze like state, or the manner in which the breeze gets the leaves in the harvest time daylight leaves you awestruck. You don't see how others aren't as moved by magnificence as you seem to be.

21. You're insightful.

Since you notice things that others miss, you're viewed as discerning and smart. Indeed, even as a kid, you may have been shrewd past your years. The world depends on exceptionally sensitive individuals like you to make it an increasingly compassionate, understanding spot to be.

THE UPSIDE OF BEING AN EMPATH

Is it difficult for you to perceive any advantage in being an Empath? Do you feel being profoundly sensitive is an issue for you? The vast majority feel that their increased mindfulness or affectability is a weight that they need it to stop and calm. It's extremely significant for you to hear how important you are as an Empath, and what number of magnificent qualities you have that separate you and give you a bit of leeway since you are profoundly sensitive.

At the point when you show signs of improvement understanding of your actual nature, acknowledge you are not the only one, begin tolerating your elevated sensitivities and afterward get familiar with the practical techniques in going to impart to you, you will have the option to progressively recognize and discharge every one of those troublesome disguised deceptions you have about how there is some kind of problem with you.

Imagine a scenario where what you accept isn't right about you was your most noteworthy limit with respect to changing the world, and you simply don't yet have the foggiest idea how to utilize your regular capacities yet.

As the greater part of you, or perhaps every one of you has finished up at once or another throughout everyday life, being exceptionally sensitive can be intense. You may feel like nobody gets you, and nobody gives you the compassion you require when something is hard for you.

There are, in reality, some extraordinary advantages of being profoundly empathic. A great many people put all the emphasis on the troubles and don't get far enough in their self-disclosure all alone to understand the tremendous advantages.

Here are the best ten reasons being an Empath is a blessing:

1. We are regular healers and can blessing healing energy to others through our hands, voices, or even by playing an instrument. Numerous Empaths decide to seek after energy healing as they feel an inward calling to recuperate themselves as well as other people.

2. Our increased feeling of smell permits us to appreciate nourishment, refreshments, blossoms, basic oils, and so forth with greater power. On the off chance that you work to build your ability of smell, you can likewise smell passing or illness in a creature or an individual. This can prompt sparing lives.

3. We will detect potential risks before others and are more on top of our intuition.

4. Since we feel everything so emphatically, we are inclined to feel further lows, yet in addition, are inclined to feel more noteworthy highs than the individuals who ate not as sensitive. The vast majority of us have an incredible eagerness forever, and experience life and bliss with more noteworthy force and will, in general, be progressively kind, understanding, compassionate, and mindful.

5. While numerous individuals who are not all that empathic feel profoundly awkward being distant from everyone else with themselves, Empaths really ache for a great deal of alone time and expect it to adjust and de-stress. We need alone time to recover, and that is not a terrible thing as we are progressively self-mindful due to this time with ourselves.

6. Empaths are strangely extremely imaginative in existence with the workmanship as well as encounters, circumstances, and potential outcomes. We think contrastingly and see things that others would not have the option to conceptualize as effectively. This imagination of thought and handling can frequently be mislabeled as off-base. However, it's really a limit of yours.

7. We can peruse emotional signs and are emotional ourselves, so we can envision well what the other individual feels and what might occur inside if this individual didn't have their requirements met.

8. Sensitive individuals are acceptable at detecting a wide range of nonverbal communication and markers of physical needs and feelings. This gives us the ability to intuiting the oblivious psyche and for detecting the requirements of the individuals who can't talk, for example, creatures, plants, newborn children, and the human body.

9. We additionally are substantially more mindful of individuals' contemplations sentiments and feelings, and on account of this, we can quite often detect when somebody is deceiving us. We know when somebody discloses to us, they are fine. However, they truly are crying within in such a case that our increased mindfulness, we can see through the bogus veneers individuals up.

10. Individuals can not mislead us without us knowing. In any event, when somebody attempts to reveal to us they are alright yet they are not, we see however the exterior they set up, and we can feel what's truly going on under the surface.

Your uplifted affectability is a blessing and not a revile. Recollect that your considerations are things, and what you believe is the thing that you make. Along these lines, next time you revile your uplifted mindfulness or affectability level recall a portion of these advantages that you've recently revealed.

By putting your emphasis on the advantages of being an Empath, you will make a real existence where your blessing is adding to you as opposed to depleting you.

EMPATH AND SPIRITUALITY

It very well may be hard from where you are present to see when your feelings will be adjusted, quiet, and gathered. It can feel incomprehensible to envision that you could recover your rational soundness or keep up a level of mental state. Have confidence that in spite of the fact that it might appear to be inaccessible, dubious, or darn close to unimaginable at this moment, that it is an unavoidable piece of this transformational venture.

Your empathic capacities may feel like they are a weight here and there, yet this is all piece of the procedure for spiritual arousing.

The main thing is this:

The vast majority of us have put some distance between our capacities to tune into the sentiments of others.

Why? Since the vast majority of us have put some distance between our capacity to tune into the sentiments of ourselves. Regardless of whether through our exceptionally emerged, quick-paced, counterfeit social orders; our since a long time ago held authoritative opinions, conventions, convictions, and internal stories; our physical and emotional eating regimens; our way of life propensities, or just our conviction that "all that we feel comes straightforwardly from us," we have been seriously desensitized throughout everyday life.

We have become basically "affectability injured."

We have become emotional, ignorant people.

Actually, the vast majority of us have become alexithymic – individuals that experience the ill effects of the failure to genuinely know and put words to what they are feeling. Subsequently, our inclination to over-eat, our weight emergency, our addictions to liquor and medications, our over-utilization of dreamer TV shows, films and pornography, and our steady psychological issues, for example, uneasiness and gloom.

The entirety of this comes as an immediate consequence of lacking self-mindfulness, of attempting to fix up the vacancy and perplexity frantically we feel throughout everyday life and inside.

We are genuine, in the most extraordinary sense, distant from ourselves.

As it's no big surprise that when we experience a spiritual arousing – when we at long last stir from our "rest" and experience a move in cognizance – we become overpowered with not just our capacity to comprehend and feel our own sentiments, however, our capacity to do moreover with others and their emotions. For some, this dives as a tsunami, for other people, a delicate, however expanding storm.

Out of nowhere, we understand up and down that many (not the entirety) of the sentiments that have been obstructing us have come because of really feeling and assuming the feelings of others, empathically.

There are a few reasons why your feelings and empathy are so sensitive during spiritual arousing. We should investigate them at this moment:

Seven Signs and Symptoms of an Empaths Powerful Spiritual Awakening

1) The inclination that something has changed within you

You can't clarify it, yet you feel unique. You even have the sensation to have become another individual, which has nothing to do with the one you were previously. The world now has another shading and another taste, essentially in light of the fact that you presently take a gander at it with new eyes...

2) Awareness of your old negative propensities

You become mindful of everything that was not directly in your "previous lifestyle," in your old you. You understand all the things you used to do and don't have any desire to do any longer, and all the reasoning examples you don't wish to keep. You are prepared for a major change, and you never need to return.

3) To not feel great with your old company any longer and to want to be distant from everyone else or with new individuals, greater arrangement with who you have become

Advancing spiritually can be an agonizing procedure, as not every person around you will advance at a similar speed. We search for new individuals, more in arrangement with who we truly are and our new energy. Normally, we are pulled in to these new individuals, who cause us to feel great and invigorated. We associate with them straightforwardly, even for all intents and purposes, as we are on the equivalent "wave-length." That is on the grounds that this time the association is from soul to soul. You "see" one another, and you are of a similar vibration. It's a substance association that is more averse to be managed by the self-image.

4) Avoid triviality and everything that isn't real

You have gotten susceptible to anything shallow and not "genuine," not valid: individuals, places, exercises, TV appears (in the event that you even continue watching it). You are on a journey to realness, effortlessness, genuine articles, that would cause your heart to sing. You may think you have gotten antisocial or "excessively troublesome," however, "it is no indication of wellbeing to be balanced to a wiped out society," consistently recall this. Continuously follow your heart.

5) Deep bitterness/compassion about the enduring on the planet

A spiritual arousing isn't generally the best inclination on the planet. It can regularly be joined by solid sentiments of gloom and trouble while turning out to be increasingly more mindful of all the enduring on the planet, even despondency for certain individuals. When we out of nowhere "see" and "get" things, it can now and again be a stun.

6) Feeling the need to improve this world a spot

Dealing with your own prosperity isn't sufficient for you. You need likewise to help other people and positively affect the world. You feel more compassion and empathy increasingly for other people and for creatures. Your life possibly has importance when you accomplish something for other people. Regardless of whether you have affected just a single individual or one creature, it causes you extraordinarily upbeat and causes you to feel as though you didn't come on earth in vain. You feel "called" to make something greater. You can't return, and in the event that you once in a while think that its difficult to be "stir," you could never need to be "sleeping" again.

7) A profound longing for importance in your life

Many things that you used to do previously are unimportant to you any longer. You need significance in your life now, else you get exhausted, and that influences you psychologically (you can even get discouraged). You have to have a reason, an objective when you wake up. You likewise need to carry out a responsibility that is significant. You can't envision yourself carrying out a responsibility that wouldn't add to the prosperity of the world.

As a spiritual empath, you might be upset by the difficulties of the advanced world. Nonetheless, it is conceivable to discover the adoration and network you long for.

Spiritual empaths need to shield themselves from the antagonism around them since they are effortlessly overpowered. Nonetheless, separating ourselves from the truth of the cutting edge world can cause an empath to feel much increasingly despondent and detached.

The battle of the spiritual empath

Spiritual Empaths regularly battle in this present reality where they believe they don't fit in. They feel the agony and enduring of the planet and don't comprehend why nothing is being done about it. This can make the empath need to pull back from the cutting edge world to abstain from invigorating their spiritual empathy.

Pulling back from the world may be valuable now and again to assist us with staying stable. Be that as it may, it can leave us feeling regretful for not accomplishing more to attempt to make the world we long for. We have to adjust our self-assurance and our movement on the planet.

Discovering balance in the cutting edge world

As a spiritual empath, it is fundamental to restrict your presentation to adverse impacts, for example, emotional reports and individuals who spout outrage and detest. We likewise need to stay away from presentation to promoting, which plays on society's feelings of trepidation so as to urge individuals to spend. Be that as it may, we additionally need to remain in contact with this world and not simply cover our heads in the sand.

Spiritual empaths are handily overpowered by the enduring on the planet and can feel miserable and vulnerable even with such should be finished. This can cause us to feel dismal, discouraged, and restless to where we are no assistance to anybody, including ourselves.

Discovering reason in the cutting edge world

One approach to discover a parity and reason for existing is to understand that, while we can't take care of the world's issues, we can have any kind of effect. We can pick a way of healing for our reality and ourselves. While we can't give all the cash and time we might want, we can pick a reason to help with our valuable time and our constrained assets.

At the point when we center around what we can do, and help ourselves to remember the great we have accomplished, this can lift the bitterness and distress and help us to feel increasingly positive even with the world's issues. Indeed, even the littlest demonstration of adoration and kindness can have a far-reaching influence on the individuals around us. Indeed, we never know when a basic kind word or deed may change someone else's life.

Searching for the positive qualities on the planet

While it is difficult to disregard the disharmony on the planet, we can likewise intentionally decide to search for the great. It assists with dodging media sources that work up outrage and contempt and spotlight on those that advance harmony, understanding, and kindness. We can look past the negative reports and spotlight on those that recount to positive accounts of mankind. By halting to wait on the narratives of individuals being caring and supportive, we can elevate ourselves.

We can likewise search for the positive qualities in the physical world around us. We can concentrate on excellence rather than offensiveness. At the point when we stop to consider the miracle of being alive on the planet in human structure, we can start to value the excursion we are attempted.

Why spiritual empaths are so significant in the cutting edge world

The astuteness of the spiritual empath is painfully required on the planet right now. We have made some amazing progress against segregation, mistreatment, and misuse. Be that as it may, there is still so far to go. It at times feels like, as a general public, we make one stride advances and afterward two stages back.

It is the astuteness of those that vibe for other people and who need to advance harmony and love that will conquer the voices of partition and abhor. Our voices should be heard. We can't all have our state in the media or legislative issues. Be that as it may, we can impact everyone around us to search for the magnificence and love no matter what.

EMPATH AND EMOTIONAL INTELLIGENCE

Emotional Intelligence and Empathy

In all honesty, these are two separate thoughts that go hand and hand, but then will, in general, be mistaken for each other. So let's take a gander at the meanings of each. Emotional Intelligence implies: portrays a capacity, limit, expertise, or a self-saw capacity, to recognize, evaluate, and deal with the feelings of one's self, of others, and of gatherings. Also, Empathy is characterized as the 'ability' to perceive or comprehend another's 'perspective' or feeling. It is regularly described as the capacity to "put oneself into another's point of view," or here and there experience the standpoint or feelings of another being inside oneself.

To give you a superior thought of the distinctions here, consider the two thoughts with regards to the artistic point of view. Emotional Intelligence would be a book written in the third individual in that it is done from the separation between one individual and another. There is no advantageous interaction here. There is no common knowledge. There is just a single individual inclination a feeling and someone else reviews and deciding that feeling structure a separation.

While Empathy would be a book in the main individual since it is truly 'placing oneself into the shoes of another' or 'seeing through the eyes of another.' One doesn't make a decision from a separation, however rather encounters the feeling both straightforwardly, however their own imaginings, and vicariously simultaneously.

Since we comprehend what each is, and their disparities, we go to a significant inquiry. For what reason do they go hand and hand? What causes one idea to neglect to work effectively without the other?

Empathy and No Emotional Intelligence

First, let's take a gander at the possibility of an individual having Empathy without the expansion of Emotional Intelligence. What this idea implies is that one has the ability to put themselves into another's point of view, yet they come up short on the capacity to decipher what they are feeling any preferable or more regrettable over the individual who is feeling those feelings straightforwardly does. It stops the procedure of empathy mostly because of the absence of understanding about individuals' feelings and the nuances of each.

In this way, for instance, if Martha is feeling discouraged due to contention with her sweetheart, the Empath can see and feel what Martha experienced. In any case, the Empath is then halted cold by their failure to decipher what they are seeing and feeling. Furthermore, in this way, along these lines, they can't see the potential results which could emerge from any guidance they may give. So they are left with a failure to pick the best game-plan when confronted with this circumstance.

Emotional Intelligence and No Empathy

Besides the conspicuous here, that the individual being referred to isn't an Empath, people are commonly equipped for extraordinary empathy, even without the title. So it is imperative to comprehend this idea, regardless of whether it doesn't concern you legitimately.

Individuals who have Emotional Intelligence, but then do not have the capacity to feel any empathy toward another person can possibly turn into a variety of things like, however not constrained to, Emotional Manipulators, Narcissists, among others. This means they can watch and evaluate someone else's feelings, yet they can not identify with it except if it, in some specific situation, has something to do with them. They learn at an early age to control the feelings of others to get their ideal reaction or their way in a circumstance. And keeping in mind that this may start as something sufficiently straightforward, such as controlling mother for $5, with age and experience it heightens as do its appearances.

The Balance of Emotional Intelligence and Empathy

For a typical individual, the adjusting of these two ideas is significant. For the Empath, it is doubly in this way, especially in the event that you are really working with others in Empathic Counseling as well as Empathic Healing Work. Since in these specific cases, you bear a duty to the individual you are helping, to give them the best consideration you can. What's more, the decision to not charge cash doesn't refute this obligation either. It's not about cash. It is about the way that, as an Empath, you hold the feelings and circumstances of another living being in your grasp, to mend or obliterate at your will, in light of your translations and decisions. Always remember this reality.

In any case, something other than that, the adjusting of these two particular thoughts makes for a lot more beneficial connections and life decisions. It offers one the capacity to see, perceive and know the various kinds of feelings, and spot themselves from another's a point of view, just for the ideal impact of having the option to pass judgment on individuals, circumstances and potential results of responses so as to pick the ideal selection of reactions.

NINE THINGS EMOTIONALLY INTELLIGENT PEOPLE DO DIFFERENTLY

High emotional intelligence (EQ) is a distinctive factor in prompting achievement. This is valid across various spaces, including a wide range of business, administration, legislative issues, training, science, and even family and social life.

High EQers do things another way.

General intelligence (g or IQ) and specialized aptitudes are the base limit necessities that you have to find a workable pace point. Past that, EQ bests IQ anytime. It's the X-factor that isolates the excellent from the normal.

Here are 9 key things that emotionally shrewd individuals do/know/comprehend about the emotional existences of themselves and of others.

1. They see what's diverse about empathy

Empathy is one of a kind psychological state. It's separated from its sister state compassion. Compassion is just the demonstration of "feeling sorry" for someone else. Empathy is considerably more fascinating: It's a suite of mental procedures that permits an individual to perceive emotional states in others, to encounter a careful match of the exact feelings and sensations felt by them, for the explanation of needing to ease the torment and enduring of that individual.

Being empathic methods that on the off chance that an individual is restless about a forthcoming presentation, at that point you're likewise on edge. You share in their uneasiness. An emotionally astute individual knows the one of a kind properties of empathy.

2. They value the different sorts of empathy

Empathy is spoken to at different levels in mind (and body). There are two sorts. The first is emotional empathy. This is the old, designed sort of empathy that lives somewhere down in the limbic locales of the cerebrum. It's the "hot" type of empathy that occurs outside cognizant mindfulness.

The second is cognitive empathy. This is the "more current" type of empathy, which is extraordinary to people (numerous other non-human creatures have a more crude feeling structure). This more up to date sort of empathy is a cognizant intentional decision – what's regularly called the point of view taking.

The fullest empathic reaction initiates both emotional and cognitive empathy. High EQ individuals understand this.

3. They know about the breaking points of empathy

All out empathy is in no way, shape, or form a panacea. Essentially having more empathy, constantly, isn't the appropriate response. A feeling of an excess of empathy can be "parochial and intolerant," bringing about "the world thinking progressively about a young lady stuck in a well than they do about the conceivable passing of millions and millions because of environmental change."

There's a period for emotional empathy, and a period for increasingly judicious, feeling free dynamic. Emotionally smart individuals welcome the points of confinement of empathy, putting it to utilize when the circumstance calls for it.

Empathy and feeling understanding are critical.

4. They comprehend the significance of feelings

Old conviction frameworks built the idea that feelings are terrible. The Stoic savants, for one, saw the "interests" as abundances of indulgence and the reason for our anguish and trouble. To them, the ethical life, easy street, was one that was liberated from feelings.

This couldn't be all the more off-base.

Brain science and neuroscience of the previous hardly any decades has, without a doubt, demonstrated that feelings are vital to essential human working. Indeed, even high request thinking and dynamic depends broadly on feelings.

5. They know the explanation behind having feelings

Some may ponder, for what reason do we have felt in the first place? What's their motivation? "feelings are for activity." All of our outward-coordinated practices are administered by the rich woven artwork of our inner emotional encounters.

Consider, for example, that the first use of feeling originated from the Latin emovir, which signifies "to move." Emotions, actually, move us. A high EQ individual knows when their practices are being influenced by an emotional state. Maybe increasingly significant, they have comparative knowledge into others' practices also.

6. They get the subtlety of feelings

Feelings go a long way past the fundamental cheerful versus tragic differentiation. They are being emotionally insightful methods having the option to attract the lines around the inconspicuous contrasts different inclination and full of feeling states. It additionally implies realizing that various circumstances will evoke these nuanced articulations of feelings and that every individual will react somewhat in an unexpected way.

The ideal approach to think about these subtleties is to consider our to be as existing inside a circumplex of measurements: an excitement measurement and a valence measurement. With this emotional guide, you can pinpoint precisely where a specific feeling sits. **For instance, a high excitement, low valence state = nervousness, alarm, dread, while a low excitement, low valence state = desolate, miserable, exhausted.**

7. They esteem negative feelings

Marking our feelings as positive versus negative is a human creation. Feelings all by themselves are neither acceptable nor terrible. They simply are. The purpose behind having a specific feeling is on the grounds that it helped our progenitors (and still encourages us today) take care of for some kind of issue. Every one of our feelings, including the negative ones, fill a versatile need.

Uneasiness, for instance, is the mind's method for saying that we ought to be extra cautious of any potential perils or dangers around us. What's more, indeed, this reaction can go haywire in certain individuals; however, basically understanding the capacity of tension can make it simpler to acknowledge and proceed onward.

8. They foresee how feelings will affect future practices

Quite a bit of our day by day life is attempting to foresee what will occur later on. We intend to settle on one choice over another; we envision a reaction from the group, or we alleviate hazard to abstain from getting singed on a monetary arrangement.

The common and low EQ individuals neglect to represent the effect that feelings will have later on, which brings about the terrible dynamic. It's a precise predisposition called the emotional determining blunder. High EQ individuals, then again, are better at arranging and anticipating in light of the fact that they realize a feeling will shading the choice or conduct. Since it generally does.

9. The name and comprehend the reasons for their feelings

The reason for an emotional encounter can be categorized as one of two classifications: coincidental and fundamental. Realizing the thing that matters is critical. An accidental feeling is a point at which an inclination that gets produced during Situation X extends into Situation Y and starts having an impact. To the less emotionally insightful people, this is a typical event and one that occurs outside cognizant mindfulness. For instance, you can identify with the tale of how an individual's displeasure after a terrible quarterly gathering gets back home with them after work.

Essential feeling, on the far edge, is the emotions that are caused in a circumstance and which an individual perceives are legitimately applicable to that one circumstance (and no others). High EQ individuals can adequately mark whether an inclination is coincidental or fundamental and improve their conduct in like manner.

THE CORNERSTONE OF EMOTIONAL INTELLIGENCE

"Put yourself from his/her perspective." That's what we advise somebody when we need them to see things from another person's perspective. Empathy is the capacity to convey (send and get messages) and lead by understanding others' contemplations, perspectives, and sentiments.

The Good Results of Empathy

At the point when empathy is improved, we become better people.

Empathy prompts:

- stronger, progressively important connections

- success in the working environment

- better wellbeing and personal satisfaction

90% of the top entertainers in the work environment have high emotional intelligence! The more individuals can comprehend their own musings, sentiments, and feelings, the more they can comprehend somebody else's. At the point when we become better audience members, we become better individuals.

The Negative Effects of a Lack of Empathy

Researchers have connected the absence of empathy to criminal practices, for example, taking, sedate managing, and murder. Our detainment facilities are loaded with individuals who need empathy. These hoodlums couldn't care less or didn't set aside the effort to comprehend what their exploited people were feeling. Having empathy may have kept them from the demonstrations that put them in detainment facilities in any case.

Trust and Openness

Empathy is the capacity to confide in others. At the point when your companions feel that you give it a second thought, at that point, you have earned their trust. On the off chance that they trust you, they will face more challenges with you and be progressively open with you. Your companions will talk straightforwardly with you just when they trust you.

As trust works, there will be all the more sharing of data, sentiments, and musings. The sharing extends the base whereupon you and others can identify with one another. In the model beneath, Susan (lady on the left) has something that is troubling her. She doesn't exactly trust Maggie (lady on the right) enough to clarify what it is.

Understanding

What do companions do as they tune in to others tell about their thoughts or interests? It's straightforward – they stop what they are doing and tune in. At the point when we are empathetic, we know about the sentiments being appeared. At the point when somebody requests help, attempt to comprehend what isn't being said alongside what is being said.

A critical part of communication is handed-off non-verbally. We may not understand it, yet we communicate something specific with each outward appearance, motion, and commotion we make. Understanding nonverbal messages is a significant piece of empathy and basic for conveying successfully. By figuring out how to comprehend non-verbal messages, we can turn out to be better at understanding how another person really feels.

Instances of Nonverbal Communication

A Solid Foundation in Emotional Intelligence Starts with Empathy

You can improve your empathy!

With training and the correct procedure, you can take your empathy to the following level, which will thusly build your emotional intelligence generally speaking. With the correct devices and assets, the procedure to learn empathy doesn't need to be confused or costly.

Other basic delicate abilities, for example, relational mindfulness, self-regard, flexibility, stress the board, and inspiration is all pieces of emotional intelligence.

EMOTIONAL HEALING

Emotional healing is a procedure. It requires various abilities. You will require some control over your consideration, the capacity to be available with the feelings you find, and the capacity to discharge them. Breath-work practice is frequently utilized. It is useful, if not required. You will likewise require the attention to watch the considerations in your mind and see that they are not valid. These are a wide range of care and mindfulness rehearses that are consolidated for emotional healing to work. Conveying emotional blockages keeps us from our spiritual excursion. Emotional healing will discharge past blockages and designs and permit significant spiritual development to happen.

Spiritual Growth

Healing ourselves emotionally is a piece of our spiritual development. Spiritual development intends to have the option to feel love, however, to communicate love without dread and judgment, to be consistent with ourselves and our wants, to follow our instinct and inward direction and follow the most elevated way, to be stirred to the soul and to live every day with adoration, harmony, and bliss.

In any case, sentiments of upliftment, delight, and association with the soul are short-lived and restricted. We have frequently encountered these sentiments during the introduction of another child, recuperation from hazardous sickness, festivities, occasions, being in nature, and meditation. These encounters can contact us profoundly and give us a significant spiritual encounter, yet what is preventing us from feeling our soul in our regular day to day existence? Can anyone explain why we feel a see-sawing of our feelings? Every so often feeling upbeat and sure and invigorated and different days have damaging idea designs, negative feelings, and feeling furious and discouraged.

To connect with our inward spiritual self, we should permit ourselves to be recuperated, not just genuinely, through doctor-prescribed medications or by attempted thorough exercise, restricted eating regimens, and intellectually through positive idea control, however on a more profound emotional level – through emotional healing.

Emotional Healing

Emotional healing permits us to grapple with occasions and conditions which have happened in our lives. When emotional healing work is done to discharge past emotional blockages, we do not just incorporate these encounters into our lives. We permit ourselves to develop and grow emotionally, on a more profound, increasingly significant spiritual level.

Emotional healing includes a combination of the divided pieces of our spirit to support us, comprehend a past encounter, however, to determine it completely, with the goal that it has no emotional reaction at all. With emotional healing, the past traumatic experience will never again control our contemplations, sentiments, and feelings. Rather, constraining conviction frameworks will be survived and enduring, positive change will happen on a more profound, soul level.

There are numerous projects, courses, and books accessible which try to enable a person to beat explicit issues, e.g., outrage the executives, increment self-regard, assemble certainty, get in shape, stop substance misuse, and so on. While a large portion of these issues can be beaten utilizing explicit strategies, it is the point at which we go further into the issue to take a gander at the reason and discharge its emotional effect that genuine change happens. Change that is transformative in nature: change that will discharge the emotional charge behind the emotional square or example.

The Mind

What number of self-assist books with having we perused, how frequently have we pledged to roll out a positive improvement towards others and not utilize outrage, to be all the more mindful and cherishing, yet neutralizing our most profound expectations there is constantly a repetitive example that makes us conflict with our best-arranged endeavors.

A large portion of us know about our cognizant considerations, and through cognizant idea control, we can impact change in our lives. Be that as it may, the same number of us have discovered, this may not prompt perpetual change. We have to go further into our intuitive psyche to life occasions that have caused distress, outrage, blame, tension, hatred, sorrow, and so forth. Any sign to us that our lives are not adjusted (e.g., high pressure, drinking excessively, eating excessively or excessively little, low self-regard, relationship or communication issues, withdrawal from others, damaging conduct and so on – even a sentiment of absence of satisfaction and absence of harmony and euphoria) means that there is some idea or memory inside the intuitive psyche that should be discharged and settled.

Any traumatic experience will stay in the body and impact the body, regardless of whether there is no cognizant memory of the traumatic occasion. An outside upgrade can trigger an oblivious response, and once there has been a trigger, there can be a comparing feeling or response to that trigger. For instance, the smell of newly mown grass on a spring day may trigger lovely and agreeable musings in certain individuals since it speaks to family life and wonderful recollections of father cutting the garden. Be that as it may, in others, it may create an alternate response, intellectually, truly and emotionally as sensitivities, cerebral pains, queasiness, distress, nervousness, and so on. The trigger was the smell of the grass, which was recognized by the intuitive brain and, in this way, caused a physical and emotional response. The curbed (or even cognizant) episode may have been the point at which an individual was explicitly mishandled, and the smell of the grass was the trigger to the memory of the occasion happening.

Since the occasion set off a past memory on the intuitive level, it very well may be hard for us to comprehend and to fathom any progressions inside the body completely, truly, intellectually, and emotionally. At the end of the day, we might be responding to natural triggers without knowing why we are doing as such. Another model would be that we become sick at a specific time every year or respond irately when certain words are utilized in our region.

An emotional memory square can be held in various pieces of the body – in the physical body including organs, tissues, and muscles, and be perceived as agony, throbs, weight, and physical ailments, for example, sensitivities, malignancy, AIDS, PMT, constant exhaustion disorder, heart issues, asthma, cerebral pains, headaches, poor assimilation, hormonal issues, synthetic irregular characteristics and so on. In the psychological body (our considerations), e.g., negative reasoning, rage, outrage, dissatisfaction, and so forth and in the emotional body, e.g., feelings, for example, distress, tension, discouragement, dread, envy and so on. These psychological, emotional, and physical examples identify with the past experience.

Emotional healing will reveal episodes that occurred in youth where it shows up there is no association with ourselves today. These previous occurrences are significant, in light of the fact that they are the impetuses in discharging examples of conduct which are influencing us regularly, responses which we could conceivably know about.

Impact on the Aura and the Chakras

Chakra is a Sanskrit word signifying "wheel." The chakras are turning wheels of energy that relate to energy focuses (called meridians in Chinese drug) inside the body. Just as the chakras contained inside our body, there is a relating energy field encompassing the body, called the emanation or auric field. The chakras and atmosphere are the human energy framework, and it is here that chi energy is caught or blocked.

The memory and the emotional effect of previous existence occasions are held inside the memory of the body, and to the prepared eye can be seen unmistakably, since they are typified inside the air and the chakras. These past encounters will prompt various types of unsettling influence inside the body, either genuinely, as agony or emotionally in an assortment of ways, dread, distress, melancholy, and so forth. This energy framework – to be specific, the chakras and emanation – hold the way to opening traumatic encounters that happened before in our lives.

Any blockage we have, regardless of whether it is originating from the brain, as out of frustration, physical as in torment or emotional as in distress, causes a discontinuity of the emanation, which may show up as spillages, gaps or sloppy spots around the quality. This discontinuity may have happened by early educational encounters and is the propelling element when we respond to anything or anybody in our condition. When the divided air is mended, we are healing ourselves truly, intellectually and emotionally, yet healing additionally happens on a spirit level, or spiritually.

Numerous types of misuse, including sexual, emotional, physical, and substance misuse addictions, including liquor, medications, and betting, can be connected to traumatic occasions held in the memory designs (frequently the intuitive psyche), which must be discharged for powerful change to happen.

When the emotional blockage is discharged, there will be a comparing emotional equalization: a sentiment of harmony, upliftment, and greatness. When adjusted, the individual will have no emotional reaction to the circumstance that caused the trauma. For instance, somebody who had encountered misuse will never again feel traumatized, restless, frightful, blameworthy, embarrassed, emotional, or irate while reviewing the oppressive episode or when seeing or finding out about comparative encounters.

Discharging the emotional square held inside the energy example of the body will likewise prompt a comparing arrival of related feelings, e.g., the most grounded felt feeling felt might be outrage, anyway the hidden feeling might be distress.

The memory of the episode is as yet held. Anyway, the emotional changes are never again present – prompting compelling and enduring change.

Emotional healing can be prompt and enduring as the change has happened not just inside the emotional, physical, and mental bodies, yet in addition to the body's energy framework: the air and the chakras, where every single past experience has been coded.

The blockage has been discharged and, in this manner, opened up the progression of energy in that chakra where it has been held and has at the same time been liberated in the auric field.

On a psychological level, since we never again hold a frightful or negative reaction to the trauma, we can make all the more effectively a future that depends on compassion, love, and wealth and not founded on the dread that the blockage, at last, speaks to.

Enduring Change

As far as healing, there is a spot for brain research and psychiatry as the two types of treatment will help the person is talking about their issues and help the individual spotlight on discovering arrangements and changing their conduct.

Healing modalities managing the physical body will likewise help discharge blockages, anyway as we recuperate the excruciating feelings and traumatic life occasions on an emotional level, we will find that change won't just be enduring, yet will carry more love and bliss to ourselves and thusly everyone around us.

It is preposterous to expect to live with unequivocal love except if we advance and work through our very own squares, which have detained the spirit. Our past encounters ought not to be viewed as impediments, for they are the encounters from which we can develop and find out about ourselves on a more profound level. It is absurd to expect to have spiritual development on the off chance that we are impervious to emotional healing.

The means we take towards understanding ourselves implies we can push ahead on our spiritual way and help other people to push ahead with their own spiritual excursion. Through this opening of our soul, we can show the way of affection, compassion, delight, and upliftment to other people.

The human psyche, characteristically fretful, triggers emotional responses when our thoughts regarding how things ought to be slam into how things are. We some of the time torment ourselves about decisions we've made, words we've spoken, and the way not taken. Or then again we harp on the future, deferring our satisfaction with musings about what is absent or wrong right now.

These contemplations and decisions are the wellsprings of our emotional agony.

The psyche has a lifetime of adapted convictions and desires through which it channels all recognitions. While the body precipitously relinquishes torment the minute the basic reason is mended, the psyche has a secretive sense for hanging on. Through the psyche, we make a jail of misery and afterward overlook that we are simply the modeler and that we hold the key that will liberate us.

Much following quite a while of emotional healing work, we as a whole here and there wrongly believe that something "out there" drives us mad, discouraged, on edge, or apprehensive. Actually, outside occasions are just triggers. The reason for each feeling is inside. By revealing the bogus recognitions that cause us to stick to torment, we can open to a profound encounter of harmony.

Practices for Emotional Release

At the point when you end up overflowed with a negative feeling, the accompanying practices can assist you with finding your way back to your center of equalization, harmony, and prosperity.

- Resist the drive to disregard your sentiments, push them away, or judge them as terrible. Rather ask them what they are attempting to let you know. All feelings – including the most troublesome ones – exist for an explanation: to support you. Will assist you with checking out the message your body needs you to hear.

- Be objective. In the event that you recognize by and by with cynicism and think, I am irate, discouraged, hopeless, worried, and so forth., it will be very hard to disengage and give up. Figure out how to consider all to be as just energy, similar to power that courses through you yet isn't about you.

- Practice self-compassion. In the event that you feel overpowered, let yourself know, "Whatever dread says, nothing can pulverize me. I'm having a solid response at this moment. However it isn't the genuine me. This also will pass.

- Take the obligation. If you end up responding to specific circumstances similarly, ask yourself what you have to figure out how to change your programmed reaction.

- Meditate. Meditation is probably the ideal approaches to extricate the grasp of clingy feelings and associate with our actual self. In meditation, we upset the oblivious movement of musings and feelings by concentrating on another object of consideration. For instance, in the act of Primordial Sound Meditation, the object of consideration is a mantra that we rehash quietly to ourselves. A mantra is an unadulterated sound, with no importance or emotional charge to trigger affiliations. It permits the brain to isolate from its standard distractions and experience the roominess and quiet inside. In the quietness of mindfulness, the brain relinquishes old examples of reasoning and believing and figures out how to mend itself.

EMOTIONAL HEALING THERAPY

When utilizing this procedure, this book will manage you straightforwardly into your intuitive where the first trauma and disarray are put away. Emotional Healing Therapy is basic and requires no uncommon capacities with respect to the customer. I am managing all of you the way. I work with you at your pace and guarantee the procedure is a safe and sustaining experience for you.

Opening the Mind: By utilizing a straightforward unwinding method, I initially interface you to your regular mindfulness, where you can watch the more oblivious degrees of your brain from a segregated, self-tolerating point of view. From that point, I securely manage you through "entryways" into your subliminal. These entryways can be feelings encompassing an issue, recollections of past encounters, or physical uneasiness. Together we can get too caught perplexity and difficult feelings and supplant this with lucidity and healing. It resembles returning in time inside your psyche, together with a talented facilitator/buddy, where you can give yourself the affection and coaching that you required at the time the trauma and resultant disarray happened.

Singular Approach: Everyone reacts to this procedure in an alternate manner. For instance, a few people discover it very simple to hold symbolism in their brains, while others react transcendently on an idea/feeling level absent a lot of symbolism. There can be a solid spiritual segment to the healing. However there doesn't need to be. It relies upon the person. The manner in which I utilize this procedure is individually focused. As it were, I connect with the manner in which your psyche remarkably works and work with you in manners that suit you best, as opposed to anticipate that you should fit into one style of procedure. The healing may include: discharging and healing old caught feelings and adjusting the mutilated recognitions that keep them caught; healing old traumatic recollections, so they never again cause you torment; increasing new understanding and insight around old and present issues that once astounded you and considerably more.

Engaging Process: Unlike hypnotherapy, While you are working with me through this healing procedure, you stay a completely cognizant member. This empowers you to find out much about how to deal with your brain, which assists with engaging you in your life's excursion.

Profound, Effective, Meaningful Healing: Emotional Healing Therapy and the 5-Step Process can create quick and compelling healing right to, on occasion, alleviating physical manifestations. Veritable and changeless healing can be accomplished with self-crushing personal conduct standards, caught emotional energy just as physical reactions. Emotional Healing is a sheltered and quick approach to manage difficult emotional issues that might be keeping you from working ordinarily and in an engaging manner. You additionally increase a lot of fundamental ability instruments that will assist you with continuing to mend and develop each day.

What can be accomplished with Emotional Healing Therapy?

- Emotional Clearing and healing

- Break old self-crushing standards of conduct

- Gently face fears and work through past trauma.

- Find lucidity of brain.

- Uncover stifled recollections

- Uncover the reason for physical illnesses

- Heal physical issues

- Connect to unqualified love and compassion

- Discover the higher importance to your life and your connections

- Connect to and cooperate with your internal identity

- Connect to and cooperate with Soul and Spirit

- Discover and experience your latent capacity

- Learn higher shrewdness

- Connect to and cooperate with withdrew friends and family

- Explore and work through previous existences that are contrarily affecting on this life.

THE WORKING PRINCIPLE OF EMOTIONAL HEALING THERAPY

Emotional Healing Therapy joins two powerful transformative strategies; NLP and EFT.

It takes a shot at the reason that the past is finished, and what stays in the psyche is all dream. In case you have dreams, you should make them great!

This beautiful articulation merits sharing: "Clutch just the recollections you'd prefer to pass onto your grandkids."

Emotional Freedom Technique takes a shot at taking advantage of the energy meridians of the body.

This by itself, discharges caught feelings, sentiments, and physical agony and is extremely ground-breaking. Regularly alluded to as "Psychological pressure point massage," the procedure works by discharging blockages inside the energy framework, which are the wellspring of emotional force and uneasiness.

These blockages in our energy framework, notwithstanding testing us emotionally, frequently lead to constraining convictions and practices and a failure to live amicably. Coming about indications are either emotional or potentially physical and incorporate the absence of certainty and self-regard, feeling stuck restless or discouraged, or the rise of impulsive and addictive practices. It is additionally now at long last generally acknowledged that emotional disharmony is a key factor in physical indications and dis-ease, and thus these systems are by and large broadly utilized on physical issues, incorporating ceaseless ailment with frequently astonishing outcomes. Thusly these methods are being acknowledged increasingly more in restorative and mental circles just as in the scope of psychotherapies and healing orders.

A short review of NLP

NLP is a conviction change framework. One of its lessons is the means by which to dismantle recollections and change them in the manner it is important to make better, cheerful agreeable ones. It might be an example of negative convictions that begins in something as basic as recalling falling into difficulty by spilling your beverage as a multi-year old. After 50 years you despite everything feeling humiliated, dumb, or futile as a result of it. It might be related to a long string of comparative circumstances which make the sentiment of being a disappointment.

Taking this one memory, we see what's going on from alternate points of view. The multi-year old you are remembering the agony. Your nonexistent parent in your mind is beating you again and again. The subliminal has related the relationship to parent with torment and outrage. At the point when you step into your mom's point of view, right now, you may find her pressure and dissatisfactions from an alternate point of view. This new understanding can be sufficient to change the memory into a positive encounter. This memory currently turns into solace, and the affiliation is acceptable. The subliminal presently connects association with affection and closeness.

The Power of Both

Joining the two methods permits us to discharge significantly more in a session than was conceivable with either apparatus all alone. We have called this Emotional Healing Therapy.

Emotional Healing Therapy

Emotional Healing Therapy deals with finding these affiliations and connects and changing them. The memory-related with the torment is changed, and the torment is discharged. Afterward, when the subliminal scans the database for past comparable encounters of irate individuals, there are none put away, and the dread response isn't cautioned. If there is no danger to our endurance, we can try to avoid panicking close by this individual in their furious state.

We can't change others' conduct. Be that as it may, when we change our own response, locate our own actual force, it changes our reality!

UNDERSTANDING THE MIND

Negative Conditioning: The psyche is, to a great extent, an assortment of encounters that go together to make up our memory arrange. This establishes our social molding and especially our convictions around self-worth. Quite a bit of our molding lies underneath our cognizant mindfulness and hues the manner in which we see and respond to the world. The majority of this is set down in our psyche before we are ten years of age. At this age, we are ignorant that this molding is occurring, and we grow up to underestimate this molding as if our molding is reality. Our emotional agony, be that as it may, is letting us know there is an issue with our molding.

We unwittingly continue showcasing this molding, which is fine on the off chance that it is positive. In the event that the molding is negative and self-damaging, it can result and numerous inadmissible life-designs, excruciating experiences, and low self-worth. The subliminal nature of our molding is the thing that makes it so difficult to comprehend and recuperate. We are so used to glancing through our molded brain. It is difficult to get above it and see it with open-minded perspectives.

Profound Trauma: At any phase in our lives, we can be gone up against with a traumatic encounter that is, at that point, past our capacity to emotionally process and put behind us. We will be unable to proceed onward until we have dealt with the effect of the trauma.

We may attempt to put it behind us, yet the experience may return years after the fact to torment our psyches as Post Traumatic Stress.

Emotional Healing Therapy has been created to empower you to pick up knowledge, healing, and the capacity to develop through such encounters, regardless of how overpowering the traumatic experience may feel to you toward the start of the procedure.

The Five Steps to Emotional healing Freedom

5 Steps for Freedom depend on a 5 stage individual procedure for emotional healing, intelligence, and strengthening.

The five stages are as per the following:

1. Acknowledgment.

2. Moral Responsibility.

3. Give up and Tune In.

4. Live in the now.

5. Live the Process as a Way of Life.

Stages 1 and 2 are the establishment of the healing and self-awareness way, whereas stages 3 and 4 spotlights further on the best way to for all intents and purposes apply these means to our own life.

This 5 stage process isn't intended to be viewed up 'til now another procedure that is superior to all the rest. Or maybe, it uncovers the fundamental rules that empower every single great procedure to work, thus improving whatever way the peruser might be on as of now.

The initial step of acknowledgment talks about how basic a key degree of self-acknowledgment and self-care is expected to start healing and self-improvement. This progression slices profoundly of healing by helping the peruser comprehend love as an unlimited all-inclusive power that can be by and by and legitimately got to whenever. This progression likewise uncovers how the human brain gets itself so confounded about adoration and endures subsequently.

The second step of moral obligation uncovers the fundamental significance of taking full responsibility to possess minds as cognizant grown-ups. Right now, peruser is stirred to the way that adoration, as a general healing power, can't be gotten to in a manageable route until we acknowledge a full duty to cherish ourselves unequivocally admirably well every day. The peruser is guided concerning how to approach this in a down to earth way where any endeavor at this grand objective is a significant encounter while in transit to turning into our very own skillful gatekeeper life.

The third step of let proceeds to tune in guides the peruser in the specialty of self-mindfulness and emotional healing. This progression shows why it is so imperative to relinquish attempting to control others in a useless endeavor to discover an asylum from dread and instability, and rather tune into what we are doing to our own self with our ongoing considerations designs. All the while, the wellspring of anguish, just as the answer for affliction, is uncovered to be inside our grip. The peruser is additionally given direction on the best way to pick up familiarity with self-crushing idea examples and work through them while managing the difficult feelings that accompany them.

The forward advance of living in the now uncovers how to get to our own capacity and push ahead in existence with the healing and mindfulness picked up from the past advances. Simultaneously, the manners in which we part with our capacity are additionally uncovered.

Stage 5 strengthens the truth that the cognizant guardianship of our own psyche is the establishment of our life. It likewise strengthens that such a procedure for healing, insight, and strengthening must turn into a focal part of our way of life in the event that we hope to conquer life's continuous difficulties and make the existence that we need.

HEALING THE HIDDEN EMOTIONS

There are times in the entirety of our lives when we end up at go across streets or defining moments. This is frequently toward the finish of a relationship when the choice to cut off that association might possibly have been made by us. Be that as it may, in any event, when the choice has been our own, this can bring about emotional disturbance and sentiments of blame and uncertainty about the insight of our choice. This sort of emotional change can likewise emerge when we arrive at a particular age, start a new position or vocation, move to start with one spot then onto the next, or even simply move home inside a similar territory, yet there are numerous circumstances all through life which bring about an emotional disturbance.

On the off chance that we are lucky enough to be encompassed by acceptable help and direction at such a period, our healing might be a normally developing procedure. In any case, whatever the underlying reason for our unrest and whether later or not, if that help and direction aren't accessible, a decent Healer can frequently assist us with finding the wellspring of stress and tension that is keeping us from living an all the more full and upbeat life.

We will obviously, in the end, arrive at where we wish to push ahead or think about entering another relationship, companionship, employment, or condition, and may discover we are experiencing issues relinquishing sentiments of agony blame and disarray. While we wish to begin over again, washed down of all the negative feelings which never again serve our prosperity, we may battle to do this. Such circumstances are perpetually connected to relationship issues, regardless of whether they are close to home or expert, old or new, and these are times when we can be at our generally helpless.

We may by this stage have re-found our idealism and eagerness, our hunger forever and our satisfaction in it, and may feel nearly inebriated with the sentiments this mixes inside us. Nonetheless, on the off chance that we were not lucky enough to have the vital help and direction from companions or family, it is frequently hard to make progress starting with one period of our life then onto the next without working from a fundamental base of dread from negative past encounters.

While those near us might be eager to help, we may feel we can't examine such issues with them, realizing that when we are prepared to proceed onward, this information is lingering palpably between us. We can be antagonistically affected without staying alert that we are clinging to fears, outrage, disappointment, hatred, failure to trust (or love) obtained en route as a technique for self-assurance. Typically these feelings are never again applicable or proper, and as we apply them to our new circumstance, they become a weight and a deterrent in the method for the 'fresh start' we look for.

Accordingly, at once in life, when we believe we ought to be at our generally happy and placated, we find we are restless dreadful and befuddled. On the off chance that we don't approach that immeasurably significant help or direction, we can bumble along in a winding of dissatisfaction disappointment and low self-regard which is self-propagating, and leaves us feeling that we are passing up an open door for future joy.

At the point when we perceive this is going on, we have ventured out our own healing procedure and will be advancing toward new and positive encounters. The following stage might be to profit by the assistance of a Therapist who can assist us with finding out of the winding and back on to the way forward. This sort of healing work can give us the private safe and nonjudgemental reality in which to examine what inconveniences us. It can likewise assist us with beginning our excursion of relinquishing those constraining feelings and recognitions we have unknowingly clutched following past troublesome or miserable encounters.

Similarly, as with other characteristic healing strategies, Emotional Healing is a nonmeddlesome procedure which basically expects you to lie back and unwind while your specialist delicately puts their hands on or over you as a rule with a blend of hands-on and hands-off work. On the off chance that you are not happy with the delicate touch once in a while utilized, you can demand that the session is finished utilizing a hands-off strategy. There is additionally no requirement for you to take off any garments other than shoes and outerwear with the goal that you can loosen up more effectively.

The Emotional Healing Process That Will Actually Make You Feel Better

Ask yourself these inquiries, and after the perfect measure of time, you'll have the option to proceed onward

After a troublesome, traumatic, or profoundly emotional experience, we're frequently left with a kind of trash, a connection to the past that chases after us.

We're spooky by thoughts of what occurred, or what could have been. The dread seeps into our present lives, and afterward forward into what's to come. We tie ourselves up and become on edge shells of the individuals we realize we're intended to be. That feeling of disappointment and disappointment just exacerbates the agony.

Emotional healing isn't caring for physical healing.

While physical healing requires rest, emotional healing requires work. It expects us to plunge into the experience, gather knowledge, and focus on completely changing us.

In the event that an emotional encounter chases after us, it must contain a message we haven't yet gotten. At the point when we can't relinquish something, this is on the grounds that we don't exactly confide in ourselves not to rehash the error. That implies we haven't scholarly, it implies we haven't developed, and the fair truth is we're in danger of rehashing history until we do.

Here's the manner by which to really recuperate emotionally:

1. Get clear on what occurred

Depict the circumstance in the least complex words conceivable. At that point, portray how you felt, and why it was so upsetting to you. Get 100% clear on the real world.

Next, go somewhat more profound. Distinguish the base of the issue just as your job in it. What was inside your control here? Where did you neglect to make a move? Where did you make an inappropriate move? What affected your activities?

Don't overanalyze, attempt to occupy, or legitimize the realities. Get clear on the truth first.

You have to give yourself a sheltered reality to encounter the full, continuous articulation of what you feel.

2. Approve your sentiments

Next, you should recognize, approve, and discharge your sentiments.

This may mean permitting yourself to cry, shake, holler, or diary about the sheer agony you're encountering. It may mean advising yourself that anybody in your circumstance would feel precisely the same way. Or on the other hand, it may mean sitting and contemplating how profoundly baffled you are and permitting that feeling to go through you totally.

You have to give yourself a sheltered reality to encounter the full, continuous articulation of what you feel.

At the point when we are frightened or upset, we will, in general, trick our ability to feel so we don't feel awkward for a really long time. What we don't understand is that we don't really stop the inclination — we simply let it wait inside our bodies.

Permit yourself to feel your legit feelings totally. This isn't just fundamental to the discharging procedure; it's likewise significant for making sense of what you should do straight away.

3. Decide a course adjustment

Last, and in particular, you should utilize the data you have assembled from the past two stages to decide how you will address your strategy later on.

Getting clear about what happened encourages you to see how to react in an unexpected way. Permitting yourself to feel the full profundity of your sentiments permits you to realize what you truly care about, the main thing to you, and what you need to make for yourself.

Concentrate on whatever something contrary to the awful inclination is. That is the thing that you truly need.

At the point when you comprehend what you fouled up, or what you truly care about encountering throughout everyday life, you're then ready to settle on choices about how to carry on. You can pick what you do and don't have any desire to do. You can figure out where to invest cognizant energy, and where to back off.

This procedure is the means by which we create ourselves. Now and then, we do it normally. On different occasions, we need a little assistance.

Whenever a staggering inclination emerges, rather than attempting to push it away, experience the way toward asking yourself: Why are you vexed, what do you truly need, and by what means will you get it going later on?

Emotional and Psychological Trauma

At the point when terrible things occur, it can require a long time to get over the agony and have a sense of security once more. However, with these self-help systems and backing, you can accelerate your recuperation.

In the event that you've encountered an amazingly unpleasant or upsetting occasion that is left, you feeling defenseless and emotionally crazy, you may have been traumatized. Psychological trauma can leave you battling with upsetting feelings, recollections, and nervousness that won't leave. It can likewise leave you feeling numb, detached, and incapable of confiding in others. At the point when awful things occur, it can require a significant stretch of time to get over the agony and have a sense of security once more. In any case, with these self-help systems and backing, you can accelerate your recuperation. Regardless of whether the trauma happened years prior or yesterday, you can roll out healing improvements and proceed onward with your life.

What is emotional and psychological trauma?

Emotional and psychological trauma is the consequence of phenomenally distressing occasions that break your suspicion that all is well and good, causing you to feel vulnerable in a risky world. Traumatic encounters regularly include danger to life or wellbeing. However any circumstance that leaves you feeling overpowered and secluded can bring about trauma, regardless of whether it doesn't include physical damage. It's not the target conditions that decide if an occasion is traumatic, however your abstract emotional experience of the occasion. The more startled and powerless you feel, the more probable you are to be traumatized.

Emotional and psychological trauma can be brought about by:

- One-time occasions, for example, mishap, damage, or a rough assault, particularly in the event that it was sudden or occurred in youth.

- Ongoing, persistent pressure, for example, living in a wrongdoing ridden neighborhood, fighting a dangerous sickness or encountering traumatic occasions that happen more than once, for example, harassing abusive behavior at home or youth disregard.

- Commonly neglected causes, for example, medical procedure (particularly in the initial three years of life), the abrupt demise of somebody close, the separation of a noteworthy relationship, or embarrassing or profoundly frustrating experience, particularly on the off chance that somebody was purposely brutal.

Adapting to the trauma of a characteristic or artificial catastrophe can introduce one of a kind difficulties—regardless of whether you weren't legitimately associated with the occasion. Actually, while it's exceptionally improbable any of us will ever be the immediate casualties of a fear monger assault, plane accident, or mass shooting, for instance, we're all routinely shelled by horrendous pictures on social media and news wellsprings of those individuals who have been.

Youth trauma and the danger of future trauma

While traumatic occasions can transpire, you're bound to be traumatized by an occasion in case you're now under an overwhelming pressure load, have as of late endured a progression of misfortunes, or have been traumatized previously—particularly if the prior trauma happened in youth. Youth trauma can come about because of anything that disturbs a youngster's feeling of wellbeing, including:

- A temperamental or perilous condition

- Separation from a parent

- Serious ailment

- Intrusive medicinal systems

- Sexual, physical, or obnoxious attack

- Domestic viciousness

- Neglect

Encountering trauma in youth can bring about a serious and durable impact. At the point when youth trauma isn't settled, a feeling of dread and defenselessness continues into adulthood, making way for additional trauma. Notwithstanding, regardless of whether your trauma happened numerous years back, there are steps you can take to defeat the agony, figure out how to trust and associate with others once more, and recover your feeling of emotional equalization.

Indications of psychological trauma

We, as a whole, respond to trauma in various manners, encountering a wide scope of physical and emotional responses. There is no "right" or "wrong" approach to thinking, feel, or react, so don't pass judgment on your own responses or those of others. Your reactions are NORMAL responses to ABNORMAL occasions.

Emotional and psychological indications:

- Shock, refusal, or mistrust

- Confusion, trouble concentrating

- Anger, fractiousness, disposition swings

- Anxiety and dread

- Guilt, disgrace, self-fault

- Withdrawing from others

- Feeling dismal or sad.

- Feeling disengaged or numb.

Physical indications:

- Insomnia or bad dreams

- Fatigue

- Being surprised effectively

- Difficulty concentrating

- Racing heartbeat

- Edginess and fomentation

- Aches and torments

- Muscle strain

Healing from trauma

Trauma manifestations commonly last from a couple of days to a couple of months, step by step blurring as you process the agitating occasion. In any case, in any event, when you're feeling much improved, you might be grieved every now and then by agonizing recollections or feelings—particularly because of triggers, for example, a commemoration of the occasion or something that helps you to remember the trauma.

On the off chance that your psychological trauma side effects don't back off—or on the off chance that they become surprisingly more dreadful—and you find that you can't proceed onward from the occasion for a drawn-out timeframe, you might be encountering Post-Traumatic Stress Disorder (PTSD). While emotional trauma is a typical reaction to an upsetting occasion, it becomes PTSD when your sensory system gets "stuck," and you stay in psychological stun, incapable of understanding what occurred or process your feelings.

Regardless of whether a traumatic occasion includes demise, you as a survivor must adapt to the misfortune, at any rate incidentally, of your feeling of security. The common response to this misfortune is misery. Like individuals who have lost a friend or family member, you have to experience a lamenting procedure. The accompanying tips can assist you with adapting to the feeling of anguish, mend from the trauma, and proceed onward with your life.

Trauma recuperation tip 1: Get moving

Trauma upsets your body's characteristic balance, freezing you in a condition of hyperarousal and dread. Just as consuming off adrenaline and discharging endorphins, exercise and development can really help fix your sensory system.

Attempt to practice for 30 minutes or more on most days. Or on the other hand, if it's simpler, three 10-minute spurts of activity every day are similarly as acceptable.

An exercise that is musical and connects with both your arms and legs, for example, strolling, running, swimming, b-ball, or in any event, moving—works best.

Include a care element. Rather than concentrating on your musings or diverting yourself while you work out, truly focus on your body and how it feels as you move. Note the vibe of your feet hitting the ground, for instance, or the musicality of your breathing, or the sentiment of wind on your skin. Rock climbing, boxing, weight preparing, or hand to hand fighting can make this simpler—all things considered, you have to concentrate on your body developments during these exercises so as to stay away from damage.

Tip 2: Don't separate

Following a trauma, you might need to pull back from others. However, disconnection just exacerbates the situation. Associating with others up close and personal will enable you to mend, so put forth an attempt to keep up your connections and abstain from investing an excess of energy alone.

You don't need to discuss the trauma. Interfacing with others doesn't need to include discussing the trauma. Truth be told, for certain individuals, that can simply exacerbate the situation. Solace originates from feeling connected with and acknowledged by others.

Request support. While you don't need to discuss the trauma itself, it is significant that you have somebody to impart your emotions to vis-à-vis, somebody who will listen mindfully without passing judgment on you. Go to a confided in relative, companion, advisor, or priest.

Take an interest in social exercises, regardless of whether you don't feel like it. Do "ordinary" exercises with others, exercises that have nothing to do with the traumatic experience.

Reconnect with old companions. On the off chance that you've withdrawn from connections that were once critical to you, put forth the attempt to reconnect.

Join a care group for trauma survivors. Associating with other people who are confronting similar issues can help lessen your feeling of detachment, and hearing how others adapt can help move you in your own recuperation.

Volunteer. Just as helping other people, chipping in can be an extraordinary method to challenge the feeling of vulnerability that frequently goes with trauma. Help yourself to remember your qualities and recover your feeling of intensity by helping other people.

Make new companions. On the off chance that you live alone or a long way from loved ones, it's essential to connect and make new companions. Take a class or join a club to meet individuals with comparable interests, interface with a graduated class affiliation, or contact neighbors or work partners.

In the event that associating with others is troublesome...

Numerous individuals who have encountered trauma feel detached pulled back and think that it's hard to interface with others. On the off chance that that depicts you, there are a few moves you can make before you next meet with a companion:

Exercise or move. Bounce around, swing your arms and legs, or simply thrash around. Your head will feel more clear, and you'll see it simpler to interface.

Vocal conditioning. As odd as it sounds, vocal conditioning is an extraordinary method to open up to the social commitment. Sit upright and essentially make "mmmm" sounds. Change the pitch and volume until you experience a charming vibration in your face.

Tip 3: Self-regulate your sensory system

Regardless of how disturbed, restless, or crazy, you feel, realize that you can change your excitement framework and quiet yourself. Not exclusively will it help assuage the tension related to trauma, yet it will likewise incite a more noteworthy feeling of control.

Careful relaxing. On the off chance that you are feeling perplexed, befuddled, or upset, rehearsing careful breathing is a speedy method to quiet yourself. Essentially take 60 breaths, concentrating on each 'out' breath.

Tactile information. Does a particular sight, smell, or taste rapidly cause you to feel quiet? Or then again perhaps petting a creature or tuning in to music attempts to rapidly alleviate you? Everybody reacts to tactile info somewhat better, so try different things with various speedy pressure alleviation methods to discover what works best for you.

You are staying grounded. To feel in the present and more grounded, you have to sit on a seat. Then, Feel your feet on the ground and your back against the seat. Check out you and pick six articles that have red or blue in them. Notice how your breathing gets further and quieter.

Permit yourself to feel what you feel when you feel it. Recognize your sentiments about the trauma as they emerge and acknowledge them.

Tip 4: Take care of your wellbeing

It's actual: having a sound body can expand your capacity to adapt to the pressure of trauma.

Get a lot of rest. After a traumatic encounter, stress or dread may upset your rest designs. Be that as it may, an absence of value rest can intensify your trauma side effects and make it harder to keep up your emotional equalization. Rest and find a good pace at the same time every day and focus on 7 to 9 hours of rest every night.

Keep away from liquor and medications. Their utilization can compound your trauma indications and increment sentiments of despondency, uneasiness, and seclusion.

Eat an even eating routine. Eating little, even suppers for the duration of the day, will assist you with keeping your energy up and limit temperament swings. Stay away from sugary and singed nourishments and eat a lot of omega-3 fats, for example, salmon, pecans, soybeans, and flaxseeds—to give your state of mind a lift.

Decrease pressure. Attempt unwinding procedures, for example, meditation, yoga, or profound breathing activities. Timetable time for exercises that bring you happiness, for example, your preferred leisure activities.

When to look for proficient treatment for trauma

Recouping from trauma requires some serious energy, and everybody recuperates at their own pace. If months have passed by and your side effects aren't easing up, you may require proficient assistance from a trauma master.

Look for help for trauma in case you're:

- Having inconvenience working at home or work

- Suffering from extreme dread, nervousness, or wretchedness

- Unable to frame close, fulfilling connections

- Experiencing alarming recollections, bad dreams, or flashbacks

- Avoiding increasingly anything that helps you to remember the trauma

- Emotionally numb and detached from others

- Using liquor or medications to feel good

Working through trauma can be alarming, excruciating, and possibly re-traumatizing, so this healing work is best attempted with the assistance of an accomplished trauma pro. Finding the correct specialist may take some time. It's significant that the advisor you pick has experience treating trauma. Be that as it may, the nature of the association with your advisor is similarly significant. Pick a trauma authority you feel great with. On the off chance that you don't have a sense of security, regarded, or comprehended, discover another specialist.

Ask yourself:

- Did you feel good talking about your issues with the specialist?

- Did you feel like the specialist comprehended what you were discussing?

- Were your interests paid attention to, or would they say they were limited or expelled?

- Were you treated with compassion and regard?

- Do you accept that you could develop to confide in the specialist?

Treatment for trauma

So as to mend from psychological and emotional trauma, you'll have to determine the terrible sentiments and recollections you've since a long time ago maintained a strategic distance from, release repressed "battle or-flight" energy, figure out how to regulate compelling feelings, and modify your capacity to confide in others. A trauma expert may utilize a wide range of treatment approaches in your treatment.

Physical encountering centers around real sensations, instead of considerations and recollections about the traumatic occasion. By focusing on what's going on in your body, you can discharge repressed trauma-related energy through shaking, crying, and different types of physical discharge.

Cognitive-conduct treatment encourages you to process and assess your musings and sentiments about a trauma.

EMDR (Eye Movement Desensitization and Reprocessing) consolidates elements of cognitive-conduct treatment with eye developments or different types of cadenced, left-right incitement that can "unfreeze" traumatic recollections.

Helping a friend or family member manage trauma

At the point when a friend or family member has endured trauma, your help can assume a vital job in their recuperation.

Be patient and understanding. Healing from trauma requires some serious energy. Show restraint toward the pace of recuperation and recollect that everybody's reaction to trauma is unique. Try not to pass judgment on your adored one's response against your own reaction or anybody else's.

Offer down to earth backing to enable your cherished one to get once more into a typical daily practice. That may mean assisting with gathering staple goods or doing housework, for instance, or basically being accessible to talk or tune in.

Try not to pressure your adored one into talking yet be accessible in the event that they need to talk. Some trauma survivors think that it's hard to discuss what occurred. Try not to compel your cherished one to open up, however, let them realize you are there to tune in on the off chance that they need to talk, or accessible to simply hang out on the off chance that they don't.

Help your cherished one to socialize and unwind. Urge them to take an interest in physical exercise, search out companions, and seek after leisure activities and different exercises that bring them delight. Take a wellness class together or set a customary get-together with companions.

Try not to think about the trauma manifestations literally. Your cherished one may lose control, fractious, pulled back or emotionally removed. Recollect is a consequence of the trauma and might not have anything to do with you or your relationship.

To enable a kid to recoup from trauma, it's essential to impart straightforwardly. Tell them that it's not unexpected to feel terrified or upset. Your kid may likewise seek you for prompts on how they ought to react to trauma, so let them see you managing your side effects in a positive manner.

How kids respond to emotional and psychological trauma

Some regular responses to trauma and approaches to enable your youngster to manage them:

•	Regression. Numerous youngsters need to come back to a prior stage where they felt more secure. More youthful youngsters may wet the bed or need a jug; more seasoned kids may fear to be distant from everyone else. It's imperative to be understanding, quiet, and soothing if your kid reacts along these lines.

•	Thinking the occasion is their deficiency. Youngsters more youthful than eight will come in general feel that if something turns out badly, it must be their issue. Be certain your kid comprehends that the person in question didn't cause the occasion.

•	Sleep issue. A few youngsters experience issues nodding off; others wake every now and again or have disturbing dreams. Give your youngster a plush toy, delicate cover, or electric lamp to take to bed. Have a go at getting to know one another at night, doing calm exercises, or perusing.

Show restraint. It might take some time before your youngster can stay asleep from sundown to sunset once more.

- Feeling defenseless. Being dynamic in a crusade to keep an occasion from happening once more, composing thank you letters to individuals who have aided, and thinking about others can bring a feeling of expectation and control to everybody in the family.

MEDITATION TECHNIQUES FOR EMPATHS

Spiritual Clearing Techniques For Empath and Sensitive People

The spiritual clearing is a term used to portray particular conduct that empaths and sensitive individuals need to receive so as to keep their energy field clean from the negative contemplations and the negative feelings of others.

On the off chance that you are an empath, you tend to detect and feel others contemplations, feelings, and even their physical agony. Contingent upon the level of your empathic capacities, you may even the interpretation of this physical torment without knowing. That is the reason energy mindfulness and establishing are fundamental elements and significant parts of energy clearing.

Energy Clearing Techniques

You can't change the way that you are an empath. This is the means by which you are made at a soul level, and you can't change this spiritual blessing. A few people talk about turning on and off being an empath, this is somewhat deceptive on the grounds that it is beyond the realm of imagination to expect to kill this capacity on and voluntarily. What you can do is gotten mindful. Being an empath is the kind of person you are, and you are here to figure out how to utilize your empathic blessing as an amazing asset for appearance and self-change.

How about we plunge into the most valuable spiritual clearing systems that are helpful as an empathy

1. Cutting The Cords

This is a significant errand that empaths need to turn out to be adept at. Since you are so acceptable at connections and individuals to love you, they additionally remove your energy from you on the grounds that your energy feels so great, healing, and cherishing. This happens on the grounds that you permitted it without knowing.

At various times associations or etheric strings with relatives, companions, and darlings can, in any case, be available significantly after the relationship is finished. It's an ideal opportunity to cut the lines!

To cut strings, essentially think about the individual with which you have had a relationship and picture the rope being cut. Favor the individual and state the accompanying: "I currently discharge you in adoration and light."

There are further developed systems on the best way to cut ropes, yet this basic technique is as compelling. My assessment is that the more we need to convolute things, the more things get muddled. It's up to you! My recommendation is to make it basic and make it simple. Be that as it may, do it and do it as regularly as you feel the need.

For instance, before nodding off every night, ask yourself: "Do I have any connections or lines with anybody that I met today?" If you discover something, discharge it and favor it.

Inquire a couple of days after the fact to ensure that the lien has been discharged. On the off chance that you don't know or feel that the string is still there, get proficient assistance. I regularly discover ropes associated with one of the chakras or connected to the energy field.

2. Clearing You Aura From Negative Thought-Forms

Your psychological body is continually interfacing with the psychological body of others, so you get contrary considerations from others.

You likewise make your own contemplations, and a considerable lot of them may not be in arrangement with your most elevated great. Know about the accompanying kind of contemplations:

- Negative

- Redundant

- Repetitive

- Automatic

On the off chance that you need to find out about your reasoning, examples convey a scratch pad with you and record all the considerations that you have inside a 24-hour time span. You will be amazed by the fact that it is so difficult to monitor your contemplations!

At the point when your considerations are certain, you adjust to positive vibrations, and you make healing, parity, and congruity. At the point when they are negative, they make obstruction and blockages.

Negative idea structures can be bolstered for quite a long time, particularly when associated with a traumatic encounter.

These negative idea structures are made by negative understanding and desires. The more energy you give them, the more energy they gain, and the more grounded their impact on your condition of parity.

They can be founded on feelings and desires for others. In any case, they can stall out in your psyche and happen again and again undetected, until you begin to focus and effectively choose to watch your idea patters.

Musings who are made out of dread, sadness, dread, fault, and outrage they stay connected to your energy field and cause you to vibrate increasingly more in arrangement with these sort of energies. After some time, they cause you to draw in these very encounters throughout your life.

These idea structures vibrate inside you so that they catalyze a fell response at all the degrees of your energy bodies: spiritual, mental, emotional, and physical. They cause you to draw in individuals, circumstances, and experiences that are in vibrational arrangement with them. It resembles a greeting for low energies to connect to your energy field.

To clear this example, take a gander at your life and check whether you are pulling in circumstances you don't care for. On the off chance that you do, you are some way or another vibrating in arrangement with them without your cognizant mindfulness.

Your errand is to check in with your energy field a few times during the day, particularly in the event that you feel drained and discouraged, to check whether you have got or made any negative idea shape and intentionally let it go.

This is the thing that I typically state:

"I am in control of my brain, my feelings, and my body."

"I am a processor, amplification, and transmuter of energy."

"I process my energy to get the hang of, enhancing the positive, and transmuting the negative."

As you state this, envision a silver-white light purging your energy field from any flotsam and jetsam of thought-frames that are beginning to grab hold. This errand will just take one moment to do.

The main thing I ask of you is to be steady!

3. Adjusting Your Chakras

Chakra adjusting for empaths is an absolute necessity, and it's a day by day practice. Two times every day, morning, and nighttimes, you have to take a couple of moments to wash down your chakras.

I like just to envision the accompanying meditation:

Envision each chakra being purged, re-stimulated and re-adjusted.

Imagine the whole chakra framework like turning wheels while permitting negative energy out of the body and positive energy inside the body.

With your brain eye, see and fell energy streaming and circling in flawless parity and agreement.

4. Make A Sacred Space

This is so significant for everybody, except particularly in the event that you are an empath. A sacred space can be any area in your home where you can be without anyone else's input and see a spot as completely self-communicated.

This could be your craft room, your meditation room, or essentially your office. This spot must be yours and yours alone. Try not to impart this space to other people (truly, your children and pets can come in and out!). It doesn't need to be inside; it tends to be outside.

Be inventive with this, however, locate an exceptional spot for you to go at any rate once per day. In the event that it is outlandish for you to make a genuine space, make one up in your mind and go there. You will be astonished by what you can make in your psyche.

A few people end up in the open country, others along the beach, a desert island, a healing sanctuary; others see themselves on different planets, out in space, or a spaceship made altogether of light energy.

5. Smearing Yourself And Your Environment

I love this part, and it is an absolute necessity, particularly when you feel down, tragic, or restless. Smirching your energy field and the earth truly assists with transmuting negative energies from your energy field.

Do this frequently, particularly in the event that you have been in circumstances that caused you to feel out of synchrony with your emotional, mental, and physical body. Utilize white sage. Likewise, remember to smear your home routinely to keep the energy of your living space new and clean.

6. Interface With Nature

For anybody who feels overpowered by emotional pressure and mental anguish, nature gives the best type of energy healing accessible. It is my conviction that empaths are here right now to help the enthusiastic frequencies important to clean the planet.

Most negative considerations and negative feelings are conveyed by people. In this way, in the event that you are an empath proceed to invest energy in nature alone at any rate once per day to energize, you will permit nature to rinse you. Contacting a tree can assist you with establishing and wipe out undesirable energies from your body.

Interfacing with creatures, blossoms, floods of water, and common scenes is the most relieving energy healing treatment you can get. What's more, it's free!

Sit on the ground with your back against the storage compartment of a tree or stroll around with exposed feet to drawn positive energies from the earth. This procedure is called establishing or earthling, and it will cause you to feel great.

7. Utilize Protective Stones

I don't accept that we should be continually worried about security since I accept that we are the main expert in our life. Accepting that we need consistent insurance can pull in the negative musings of debilitation, dread, and victimhood.

So as to ensure your energy field, you should know about your energy.

I do accept that empaths need to discover approaches to keep themselves grounded and washed down constantly. This is, as I would like to think, the best type of assurance.

After the Heart-Wall clearing, it's imperative to put a shield of security around the hear so as to keep the heart totally protected and ensured negative structure energies and consistently in arrangement with positive energies. When you have cleared your Heart-Wall and put a shield of assurance, you should simply initiate your shield.

At the point when I work with individuals, I educate basically energy strategies that they can use to ensure their auric field. However, I don't advance the requirement for insurance as much as the requirement for energy mindfulness.

At the point when we are intentionally mindful of our energy, we can't fall casualties of others except if we permit it. Your energies should be continually moving in doing what we are here to do as empaths: process, transmute, and enhance energy. On the off chance that you are not doing this throughout the day, you will feel dormant energy. Regularly time, this is the motivation behind why you fall back into the negative part of your blessing and feel the requirement for assurance.

In this way, working with gems and stone causes you to remain focussed and mindful of what's happening in your life. This isn't anything but difficult to do when you are out there, in reality, making your background. Be that as it may, you need not free core interest. Be over your energy!

Obsidian stones are awesome repellants of negative energy. You can keep them in your pocket or satchel.

Dark Obsidian is valuable in purifying your auric field from cynicism. It is utilized to battle off the mystic assault.

On the off chance that you do spiritual healing work, this gemstone can assist you with establishing you to the planet Earth.

Wash down your stones every now and again and program them for healing and insurance.

8. Use Journaling, Art, and Drawing

Empaths will, in general, be exceptionally creative and love communicating their own ability when they feel incredible. At the point when they don't feel incredible, they will, in general, oppose their imaginative capacities since workmanship necessitates that they work with their emotions, and this can regularly cause torment.

I welcome you to think about utilizing workmanship as a type of healing and emotional discharge to help you when you feel stuck and out of equalization.

9. Cry As A Form Of Emotional Release

Empaths have a refined emotional body, and they have to cry when they want to do as such. Crying has such a large number of healing advantages. The vibration of crying fills in an as purifying instrument for your atmosphere. Youngsters do this constantly.

Doing Yoga, Tai Chi, or different types of energy development can be extremely useful to help discharge pressure, let go of undesirable negative energies, purge the atmosphere, and realign the body and chakra framework.

Additionally, doing energy work is the ideal approach to keep your emanation washed down and in amicability with your spirit's way.

10. Ocean Salt Baths

Ocean salt has astonishing purging capacities. Ocean salt coaxes energy out. Having a hot shower containing ocean salt when you feel enthusiastically overpowered can truly have a colossal effect in the manner you feel. You can utilize ordinary ocean salt, Himalayan salt, Epsom salt, or other.

You can likewise include a couple of drops of basic oil to the water. On the off chance that you have sensitivities, try to test them first. The best basic oils to use for purifying the emanation are rosemary, citronella, and eucalyptus.

Which Energy Clearing Technique Is Best For You?

I would urge starting today to receive a portion of these techniques and test with them. Perceive how your body feels. Focus on your feelings and considerations. Tune in to your body, what messages is your body sending you? Know about what's going on in your condition.

Notice what individuals state around you and what you state around them and what sort of discussion you are taking part in. Your outside experience is constantly an immediate appearance of what's going on in your psyche.

In the event that you feel overpowered and need some lucidity, you may have caught feelings. It's an ideal opportunity to discharge them!

We, as a whole, prefer to see ourselves as decent individuals. We like to imagine that when given a decision among good and bad, compassion, and lack of interest, we'd pick the alternative that is accommodating to other people. Present-day superheroes make the rounds in viral recordings praising acts like paying for the outsider behind you in the drive-through or conveying a little creature from a hazardous area.

In any case, we should be sensible: we're occupied, surged, and focused on species. At the point when a colleague gets some information about something we've just explained multiple times (and again in an email), we may snap. Getting disappointed moving around an individual gazing at their telephone in the focal point of the basic food item passageway or proceeding with a lively pace as opposed to helping a bystander battling with their packs doesn't make somebody a "signify" individual. Yet, consider the possibility that we could really prepare ourselves to react to these situations with more compassion. An examination utilizing Headspace shows that it may be conceivable.

Meditation is presently generally known to affect a person's emotional wellness and bliss positively. Shouldn't something be said about its effect on the individuals around us, meditation's impact on prosocial conduct—conduct that is expected to be certain, useful, or amicable to someone else? Would somebody rehearsing meditation be bound to loan some assistance to a more bizarre than a non-meditator?

A gathering of 56 members was arbitrarily doled out to one of two exploratory conditions. One gathering was to finish a three-week care meditation preparing to utilize Headspace, while the control bunch was to finish three weeks of an electronic "mind games" program, which was likewise self-guided.

After each gathering had effectively finished their sessions over the multi-week time span, they were welcomed to the lab's holding up the region, which had three seats, two of which would as of now be involved by additional items advised to remain in their seats. The members would sit down in the final seat. Subsequent to sitting for one moment, a third extra would go into the room, strolling with supports and a medicinal boot and showing obvious distress.

Here was the genuine test: would the member offer their seat to the tormented individual on props, or sit idle? Offering the seat, obviously, was viewed as the more compassionate reaction right now. Members who had finished care preparing with the Headspace application surrendered their seats more frequently than those doled out to the control gathering.

In any case, it reaffirms past discoveries that meditation and care can elevate compassionate conduct expected to profit others.

Anyway, what could this mean for all of us? To a great extent, these discoveries illustrate what an increasingly compassionate society could resemble. On the off chance that three weeks of 10-

minute meditation practices prompted an expansion in cordial and supportive conduct, it's not hard to envision what care for an enormous scope could mean for our networks.

At the point when we're given grace from others, we're bound to "show proactive kindness." We may be bound to help out an outsider out of luck, urging them to spread some liberality too. Outsiders with fiercely various sentiments may delay assuming the best about one another. Understudies could get more empathy from their instructors, shaping more quiet connections in schools. The manner in which compassion spreads could seriously affect the manner in which our days work, facilitating the Headspace crucial, improving the wellbeing and joy of the world.

Meditation could help individuals to be progressively empathetic, as per a little new examination from Emory University.

A meditation program called Cognitively-Based Compassion Training had the option to improve individuals' capacity to peruse emotional demeanors on others' countenances. Scientists said the meditation program depends on antiquated Buddhist practices, yet this specific program was mainstream. It included care procedures; however, basically included preparing individuals to consider their associations with others.

"It's an interesting outcome, proposing that social mediation could upgrade a key part of empathy.

As fMRI cerebrum filters as they were regulated, a "Guessing the Thoughts in the Eyes" test to measure empathy. The test includes taking a gander at highly contrasting photos of various outward appearances - with the exception of the photos just shows the eye district of the face. Individuals stepping through the examination are then solicited to state what kind from feeling or believing is being evoked in every articulation.

In the meantime, individuals who just participated in the conversation classes didn't encounter any expansion in empathy scores, and some even encountered a reduction in their scores.

The cerebrum filters additionally uncovered that individuals who took the meditation courses likewise had expanded mind movement in the locales connected with empathy.

Empathy is significant and not just for supporting relational connections.

SAHAJA MEDITATION

Sahaja meditation improves every one of our connections by helping us develop and sustain emotional characteristics, for example, empathy, compassion, and kindness. These characteristics help move our point of view from self-situated to other-arranged, balancing the normal human propensity to act naturally focused. We realize that, for the duration of our lives, the capacity to comprehend and share someone else's experience is formed by understanding and condition, yet is there a genuine physiological reason for empathy and compassion? All things considered, numerous investigations have indicated that comparative neurological action can be found in the cerebrums of both an individual who's in torment or trouble and an individual who's only seeing their torment. Are a few of us designed for it and a few of us not?

Empathy Begins at the Cellular Level

In the event that you've at any point viewed a motion picture and strained, jumped or recoiled when the lowlife raises a blade to slice somebody, that is your mirror neurons terminating.

Mirror neurons are particular nerve cells in the separate district of the mind's frontal cortex that create empathy.

In that brief moment, you can see how that poor injured individual feels — maybe it's transpiring.

Mirror neurons were incidentally found in the mid-1990s. Giacomo Rizzolatti and a group of Italian neuroscientists were contemplating monkey mind frameworks that regulate purposeful hand developments and found an arrangement of neurons that represent considerable authority in the "strolling from another's point of view" work. They found that neurons in the premotor zones of the frontal cortex that prime development successions, (for example, getting a handle on an item) were really enacting milliseconds before the hand development had even happened. These mirror neurons likewise initiated when the monkeys just watched another monkey making that equivalent development grouping. Maybe the monkeys were impersonating — reflecting — another's developments in its brain.

We people have an amazingly unpredictable mirror neuron framework that includes our whole tangible framework and permits us to reenact the emotional existence of others. Mirror neurons additionally work as a cognitive subsystem that empowers the psyche to recreate and afterward impersonate the watched development successions of others. So notwithstanding framing the natural premise of empathy, reflect neurons may likewise shape the premise of scholarly, imitative, and infectious practices. These administrative frameworks are accepted to grow very quickly in child practices, particularly infectious practices, for example, an infant reacting to a snicker with a chuckle, as right now of quadruplets giggling at one another, which may trigger some infectious chuckling from you, as well.

In emotional viruses, we "get" a feeling from someone else at a subliminal level. Be that as it may, numerous development abilities can't be exclusively educated through a virus or through verbal guidance, as any individual who's at any point attempted to enable an infant to figure out how to walk or encourage a kid to ride a bike knows. Frequently, impersonation is the best educator. What's more, that applies to moral practices, too.

Kids gain empathy best from guardians who respond empathically to other people. The exercise is progressively impactive when empathy is illustrated, as opposed to simply "educated."

Reflecting empowers us to "read minds" and anticipate others' expectations or practices, which may help clarify the expansive intrigue of watching virtuoso exhibitions by other people who are occupied with, for instance, sports, movie, or music. We appreciate watching and foreseeing their developments, and in our brains, maybe, it seems as though we are performing ourselves.

In this way, on account of mirror neurons, every single social creature — from canines to people — might be designed for empathy, while retaining and coordinating social and ecological impacts en route.

The mirror neuron framework is by all accounts included not in the reasonable kind of empathy associated with intentionally envisioning yourself from another's point of view; however, in the profound, programmed empathy of truly feeling what someone else is feeling.

Be that as it may, what happens when something turns out badly with the mirror neuron framework? Autistics, for instance, don't be able to comprehend, from watching others, what it feels like to be miserable, irate, sickened, or astonished, nor do they normally get a handle on the hugeness of those feelings. An investigation distributed in the January 2006 issue of Nature Neuroscience found that breaking down mirror neurons assume a focal job in the medically introverted youngster's social segregation or powerlessness to associate. Mentally unbalanced youngsters are, generally, unfit to make self-cognizance. Hence they can't find incapable of comprehending the awareness of others.

However, analysts are putting forth a coordinated attempt to investigate meditation as a technique to supersede breaking down mind frameworks and the weakening manifestations of chemical imbalance. Late research recommends that meditation may demonstrate compelling for autistics at both the social and atomic levels. Mantra meditation, specifically, has been seen as helpful in youngsters somewhere in the range of 3 and 14 years old.

In the event that meditation can improve empathy and compassion in people who have had, from birth, practically zero limits with respect to empathy and compassion, envision what it can accomplish for all of us.

Compassion has been portrayed as having a transmitting impact, spreading kindness and pardoning to other people, even the individuals who have treated us gravely. Along these lines, compassion can possibly kill a craving for hostility, discipline, or vengeance. Meditation successfully fortifies self-control and character improvement at the same time.

Meditation Enhances Empathy and Compassion

Care can work as "empathy preparing," and care can be created through meditation. Care has been appeared to expand a few parts of compassion and empathy, particularly point of view taking and empathic concern. Attunement, which is a part of care, assumes a basic job. Empathy and compassion rise up out of attunement to oneself and to other people. The capacity to concentrate on and interface with the psyche of someone else draws in neural hardware that empowers two individuals to "feel felt" by one another, to reverberate with the inward universe of another, to feel associated. Youngsters need empathic attunement to have a sense of safety and to grow well. Grown-ups keep on requiring attunement for the duration of their lives to feel close and associated.

Sahaja meditation study utilizing the cerebrum structure imaging strategies of MRI and Voxel-Based Morphometric found that long haul Sahaja specialists (contrasted and non-meditators) had fundamentally bigger dim issue volume in the left ventrolateral prefrontal cortex and left insula. These are areas related, to some extent, with emotional intelligence — just as in right hemispheric locales (insula, ventromedial orbitofrontal cortex, mediocre fleeting, and parietal cortices) related with, among different qualities, sentiments of empathy, compassion, and philanthropy.

Extended dark issue volume right now the correct transient flap is related to socio-emotional capacities, for example, more prominent empathy and deciphering the goals of others, significant limits that encourage the feelings of adoration and compassion.

The finding of amplified dim issue volume in Sahaja professionals recommends that the long haul practice of Sahaja may build neuroplasticity, in this manner improving our capacity to proceed with increment empathy and compassion after some time.

Another late fMRI examines discovered that meditation upgrades the inclination to react to someone else's hints of misery or agony. Meditation may change the actuation of mind hardware connected to empathy, which impacts our capacity to develop positive feelings. What does empathy resemble in the cerebrum? Right now, amateur and experienced meditators demonstrated an expanded empathy response when in a thoughtful state. In any case, fMRI sweeps of experienced meditators uncovered a lot more prominent movement (contrasted with tenderfoots) in mind organize that regulates empathy (insula and front cingulate cortices) in light of human emotional hints of trouble and expanded action in cerebrum locales recently connected to mentation (thought) about the emotional conditions of others. Experienced meditators additionally exhibited a lot more noteworthy capacity to recognize emotional sounds and deliberately produce compassion.

The more profound and progressively exceptional our meditations, the more prominent our ability for empathy and compassion.

What's the contrast between empathy and compassion?

Empathy and compassion are regularly conflated. However, they are really various characteristics. Being empathetic doesn't really that you are compassionate. Empathy is the capacity to comprehend the sentiments of others and even sympathize with their agony while staying alert that it's another person's feeling.

Empathy isn't characteristically acceptable or star social. It's ethically nonpartisan.

For instance, skilled insane people are fit for empathy, yet they regularly utilize that information and understanding of others' feelings to control them. So despite the fact that they have empathy, they need compassion.

Compassion is empathy (the capacity to comprehend and share others' sentiments) in addition to compassion or concern and maybe, in any event, feeling the torment of others when we see them languishing. Empathy is a forerunner to compassion that ideally prompts compassionate activity that may mitigate another person's misery.

Empathy gives the straightforward affirmation "you are not the only one." Compassion is kindness in real life.

Would we be able to prepare ourselves to be compassionate through meditation?

Research recommends that we can, much the same as we can figure out how to play an instrument or create explicit athletic aptitudes. fMRI examines discovered that compassion meditation — concentrating on compassion and empathy for others during meditation — builds empathy. Compassion meditation enacts zones of the limbic (emotional) framework (the insula and worldly parietal point, which are associated with empathy and feeling sharing, remembering recognizing emotional states for other people) in both fledgling arbiters and priests (Lutz et al., 2008). Another investigation found that only four minutes of meditation brought about expanded sentiments of social connectedness and inspiration toward outsiders.

How empathy and compassion shows in Sahaja

The bedrock of Sahaja meditation is the amazing female energy of Kundalini that is stirred during the Self-Realization process. When stirred, the Inner self joins with the all-overrunning astronomical energy of the universe.

Intrinsically, both these energies speak to the intensity of adoration and compassion. In that sense, you accomplish the intensity of affection and compassion intrinsically on day 1 of the act of Sahaja meditation.

This resembles how the motor that is fitted in the vehicle is a definitive main thrust and the explanation behind its reality, its motivation, and utility. Self-Realization or commencement into Sahaja meditation in this manner stirs the principal intensity of our reality, the intensity of affection, and compassion.

The appearance of compassion, to an enormous degree, is characteristic and inherently settled once you begin rehearsing Sahaja meditation. This implies you'll feel a programmed, intrinsic sentiment of empathy – elevated mindfulness and thought of the earth and individuals around you and compassion – the craving to be caring and accommodating to them consistently. This likewise implies Sahaja meditation is far better in the capacity than create and increment compassion as it needs next to no concentration or express preparing – the more you draw upon the energy inside, the more compassionate you can turn into.

Additionally, this sort of compassion is anything but a psychological exercise of attempting to creating compassion or a psychological note to oneself to be thoughtful others. You feel kind and compassionate from inside, commonly to your own shock. With every meditation session, your association of the energy to the all-overrunning power gets solid, and subsequently, the compassion additionally gets more grounded and progressively dug in inside you.

As you progress in the excursion of Sahaja meditation, there is the further fortification of the nature of compassion by improving your fourth energy place, the heart chakra.

Since the intensity of compassion is the main impetus in Sahaja, it additionally establishes the framework for creating different characteristics. Absolution is improved as we feel more noteworthy compassion towards others and a superior understanding of the missteps they make.

Three Meditations that Cultivate Compassion

Developing compassion can assist you with remaining present with the enduring you're confronting every day—without getting overpowered. Here are three meditations to assist you with reinforcing your compassion muscles, so you're set up to meet the enduring you witness.

Have you winded up posing this inquiry significantly more of late? Ongoing extraordinary climate occasions have dislodged a great many individuals around the globe. Shocking savage scenes are tormenting honest individuals. Displaced people and workers face vulnerability, and worldwide tact issues keep pressure high.

Once in a while, you may feel incapacitated and unfit to make a move, and that is a typical response. You may feel that you can't shoulder the heap of enduring that is dumped upon you without fail. By rehearsing compassion development meditation procedures, you can figure out how to remain present with the enduring you're confronting every day without getting overpowered. You can prepare your psyche to communicate empathy for that outside of your typical hover of compassion and figure out how to rehearse compassion for yourself.

Here are a couple of compassion meditation practices to assist you with fortifying your compassion muscles so that during intense conditions such as these, you're set up to meet the enduring you witness.

1. Adoring Kindness or Metta Meditation

You can utilize a basic cherishing kindness or Metta meditation to assist you with rehearsing compassion for individuals who are outside of your ordinary in-gathering. For the most part, Metta meditations start with offering compassion toward yourself and afterward extending that outward to companions and friends and family, and, at long last, to individuals you may not know. You can likewise utilize this training to create compassionate sentiments toward somebody who disappoints or rankles you.

- Begin by finding an agreeable position that permits you to be alert yet loose. Take a couple of full breaths to settle your psyche and ground yourself.

- Next, rehash the accompanying expressions in your brain: "May I be cheerful. May I be tranquil. May I be liberated from misery."

- As you state each expression in your brain, check whether you can envision breathing warmth and compassion into your heart space and afterward breathing out warmth and compassion toward yourself, letting the compassion penetrate your body.

- Next, direct those equivalent expressions to somebody who is of high repute to you, saying: "May you be upbeat. May you be quiet. May you be liberated from anguish."

- Finally, pick an individual or a gathering you don't know well. Maybe, it's a neighbor who you see however don't know well. On the off chance that you've revealed your oblivious predispositions, you can rehearse compassion for the individuals who you might be verifiably judging, similar to a specific sex, ethnicity, sexual direction, or body type.

- Again, rehashing the expressions for this individual or gathering: "May you be glad. May you be quiet. May you be liberated from affliction."

This basic practice is utilized by analysts to produce constructive feelings and furthermore has been appeared to diminish verifiable inclination toward demonized outgroups like dark individuals and vagrants.

2. Self-Compassion Meditation

There are a few kinds of self-compassion meditations, and I suggest you discover one that best suits you. The underneath training utilizes a smidgen of slyness to assist you with creating sentiments of compassion for yourself. One major obstacle for some individuals right now conjuring the sentiment of compassion for self. This training permits you to initially associate with the sentiment of compassion for another person, which you would then be able to coordinate toward yourself.

- Find an agreeable, upstanding position. Tenderly close your eyes and take a couple of full breaths, breathing in through the nose and breathing out through the mouth.

- Return to your typical breathing pace and focus on your breath for a couple of moments. This will help settle the psyche. At the point when you notice your brain meandering, which it will tenderly take it back to the breath.

- After settling the psyche, envision a friend or family member remaining before you. Focus on how your body feels when you are with the person in question; attempt to concentrate on any warm or constructive sentiments.

- Imagine sending affection, warmth, and light out of your heart to your adored one with each breathes out. Saying as far as you could tell to your adored one, "May you be glad. May you be serene. May you live easily."

- Now envision seeing yourself by your adored one. Direct that equivalent warmth, light, and love from your heart to that picture of you, quietly saying, "May you be upbeat. May you be quiet. May you live effortlessly."

- You can transform this into a Metta practice by broadening adoration, light, and warmth with each breathes out, sending it to the individuals from your local, state, country, mainland, lastly to everybody on the planet. Saying quietly to each gathering, "May we as a whole be cheerful. May we, as a whole, be serene. May we as a whole live effortlessly."

3. Tonglen Meditation

Tonglen is a representation practice utilized in Tibetan Buddhism, and it signifies "giving and taking." Simply put, you utilize your breath to take, or breathe in, the enduring of somebody, and you give, or breathe out, compassion.

- To start, locate an agreeable position permitting you to feel loose yet alert. Subsequent to taking a couple of purifying breaths, follow your breath and settle the brain for five minutes.

- Next, infer an individual who is encountering enduring, and envision he/she is remaining before you. Envision his/her enduring as a foreboding shadow encompassing him/her.

- As you breathe in, envision taking in obscurity cloud. As you inhale it in, the cloud changes into a splendid, warm light of compassion at your heart region.

- When you breathe out, you stretch out that light of compassion to him/her, reducing his torment.

- Continue taking in obscurity haze of affliction, permitting the cloud to change into warm, brilliant light, and guiding your compassionate warmth to your cherished one as you breathe out.

- When you are prepared to come back to the present minute, take a couple of profound, careful breaths.

This training feels overpowering for certain individuals, so make certain to practice alert while attempting it. On the off chance that you think that its hard to take in a foreboding shadow, you should try different things with envisioning the foreboding shadow as a white or splendidly hued cloud or as cool air.

Tonglen is another most loved on-the-spot practice, and it's an incredible device to keep in my back pocket. You can utilize it to remain present when you witness or experience languishing. You have envisioned a foreboding shadow of enduring over those influenced by catastrophic events. Take in that cloud and inhale out compassionate light. At the point when I am up close and personal with an individual who is enduring, I utilize tonglen to assist me with remaining present when I may have, in any case, felt overpowered.

Notice what happens when you incorporate compassion rehearses in your collection of meditations. My expectation is that they bring you and numerous others harmony during troublesome occasions.

CONCLUSION

People are completely fit for incomprehensible brutality. That horrible nature knows no limits, and individuals result in reprimanding, annoying, harassing, ambushing, slaughtering, and tormenting one another, and that's just the beginning.

This book has extensively characterized what empathy is and who an empathy is, and can be utilized to portray a wide scope of encounters. This book has isolated this general definition between two distinct kinds of empathy: Cognitive and Affective.

Cognitive empathy can likewise be portrayed as viewpoint taking, and it references our ability to comprehend and recognize the particular feelings of others. Individuals with Autism have an especially troublesome time with this particular empathetic sort. Full of feeling empathy references our capacity to encounter the sentiments or vibes that are ordinarily activated because of the feelings of others. Specifically, this kind of empathy is confirmed in one of two different ways. The principal way includes the presence of a sentiment of worry because of the dread or nervousness of someone else. The subsequent method to show full of feeling empathy is to reflect the other individual's feelings back to them.

From a less specialized viewpoint, empathy is just the capacity to comprehend someone else's perspective. That understanding is the establishment of communication, regard, and profound quality.

CPSIA information can be obtained
at www.ICGtesting.com
Printed in the USA
BVHW091347220321
603178BV00007B/548